FROM

Social

TO

Sales

We would like to dedicate this book to our families
and to all that supported us in bringing this project to reality.

We would like to acknowledge Matt Hoffer for the excellent cover and interior design; Matt Holman, LaQuenda Jackson, Mark Macesich and Stanley (Sonny) Bynum Jr. for reviewing and suggestions; and Laurie Kight for editing this book.

FROM SOCIAL TO SALES:
THE AUTO DEALER'S GUIDE TO NEW MEDIA

By Douglas DoNascimento, James Mayfield and Cheran Ratnam

Published by Briggs & Schuster BSA.IM

Copyright © 2014 by DoNascimento.com/Books

Library of Congress Cataloging-in-Publications is available

ISBN: 978-0-9835120-2-8

First Edition, 2014

Printed in the United States of America

About the Authors

Douglas DoNascimento

Douglas DoNascimento is an early adopter of social media and a graduate of marketing from SMU. With more than 17 years of experience, he has envisioned, created and implemented digital strategies for many local, national and international organizations. He's been recognized for his accomplishments through awards including two Press Club of Dallas Awards, The Best in Class and Best Mobile Website Awards from Greystone, two Bravo Awards, Advertising Award, Horizon Award, Web Awards, Aster Awards, Internet Advertising Competition Award, and 15 other industry recognized awards. This is the third book from DoNascimento. Currently he leads the social media marketing team for one of the top 10 auto loan banks in the world.

James Mayfield

James Mayfield comes from a "car family." Some of his fondest childhood memories center around the dealership run by his grandfather and uncle in Oklahoma. As a writer and editor, his work has appeared in the pages of several publications including *Esquire, Non-Prime Times, Paste, Success, Virtuoso Life* and *Celebrated Living.* A former editor with *American Way* magazine, Mayfield earned a bachelor's degree in communications from the University of Missouri and makes his home in Fort Worth, Texas, where every month is "Truck Month."

Cheran Ratnam

Born in Dallas and raised in Sri Lanka, Cheran grew up in the lush mountains of Central Sri Lanka playing rugby and cricket. He finished high school in his mother tongue, Sinhalese, before moving back to Texas. Initially embracing social media to keep up with his scattered high school friends, he soon developed a niche for utilizing social media to reach diverse audiences. While in Texas, he majored in journalism (M.A) at the University of North Texas and earned his B.A in anthropology from the University of Texas, Austin.

CONTENTS

INTERMEDIATE

ADVANCED

APPENDIX: LOOKING TO THE FUTURE

SOCIAL MEDIA: WHAT AND WHY

SOCIAL MEDIA. The big picture. The real deal. The open highway. Regardless of how you refer to it, the fact is that there are literally thousands of social media channels available. These channels continue to grow in leaps and bounds with newer channels popping up daily to compete for the attention of billions of social media users. In *From Social to Sales - The Auto Dealer's Guide to New Media*, we focus on the top social networks that are most valuable for building your automotive business. Whether you are a green-pea or a shark or anywhere in between, our goal is to equip you with knowledge that will help leverage your odds in the highly competitive automotive business.

This book answers questions like, What is social media? Why do you need social media? Where should you start? How do you make money using it? How do you measure your success in social media?

What is "social media"?

It's more than just being social.

More than just media.

Or marketing.

We call it ... relationship networking.

"Social media" describes marketing methods used to reach users who choose to use an Internet location as a communication tool. It's a bulletin board, photo album, chat room, water cooler and workplace lunchroom all rolled into one. For you, the key role of social media will be reaching specific audiences with specific messages at specific times.

Let's use a football stadium as an analogy. Inside the stadium, fans of both teams fill up the stands and cheer for either of the two teams. Football fans come in different shapes, ages and sizes and represent different professions, races, geographic regions, experiences, etc. Say you want to specifically communicate with fans from only one of the teams and who are senior citizen doctors and lawyers; social media is a filter you can use to remove everyone else from the conversation.

As you can imagine, the point is not to simply be social, to push some sort of new medium, or to sell, sell, and sell ... it's about building advocates for your brand, i.e. your dealership. It's about creating trustworthy and transparent relationships that will compel your audience to engage, and stay engaged, with your brand. Your goal should be to casually interact with your customers online, just like you would in person. Here's why: Consumers are smarter in their automotive research than they have ever been and chances are that before they head over to your lot to buy a car, they will research your brand (dealership) via social media. If you're not engaged in social media, a savvy consumer will be more cautious about doing business with you. In the digital age, you need to be involved with social media to grow your business.

Social Media Simplified

Below is a summary (from the consumer's point of view) of what each social media outlet offers.

Facebook: "I am going to buy a car this weekend, but I am between a Honda and a Ford, which do you think I should buy?"

Twitter: "On my way to buy my new car!"

LinkedIn: "Car buyers wanted. Apply online."

Google+: "I went to test-drive the new Ram truck, but I can't decide on which one to choose. Here are the photos. Please help me decide!"

Skype/Facetime/Google Hangout: "Here's a live walk around of the car you are looking to buy online."

Blogs: "Car-buying tips - These are my favorite tips for buying a used car."

Yelp: "After reading these reviews, I am certain that I will be buying from Dealer X."

YouTube: "Here is a video of me driving my new car."

FourSquare: "Checking-in at my local dealer."

Flickr: "My new ride photo gallery."

Delicious: "My favorite car dealer bookmarks."

Pinterest: "These are my dream cars."

Instagram: "Here is my classic ride vintage style."

Within each of these environments, you can drill down further and focus your efforts and dollars on creating meaningful interactions with the right audience at the right time.

In the coming sections, we will define each of these channels in more detail. We will also provide suggestions for auto dealers as beginner, intermediate and advanced social media users.

The great news is that there are very few mistakes you can make in the online world that you can't fix. However, if you choose to ignore social media, you will miss many, many, many (did we say many?) potential buyers.

QR CODES (SEE PAGE 41)

Download a QR Code reader and point your smartphone to QR Codes provided throughout the book to access additional information, videos, images, etc. Using QR Codes is fun and is a great way to provide additional information. We will discuss how you can use QR Codes in your social media campaigns later.

WHY SOCIAL MEDIA

AS YOU HAVE PROBABLY NOTICED, social media is not a fad. It's everywhere and it's here to stay. As an auto dealer, how can you get the most out of it?

For starters, you can use social media as a lead-generating tool to keep your customers and prospects engaged. It's also valuable when used to increase customer satisfaction and loyalty, which in turn, drives word-of-mouth referrals creating advocates for your dealership.

Social media can also be used to build and retain audience relationships. If you listen and respond to inquiries, you will gain valuable insight into the minds of your prospects and customers. Unlike other marketing tools, it's not only about sales. In fact, if all you do is promote products and prices, you will most likely fail in the social media world. When it comes to social media, relationship building is the key that will turn mere users into lifetime advocates.

There was a time when email campaigns, hard copy marketing materials and newspaper ads were enough. Heck, you could even blow up balloons and tie them to bumpers to make sales. Times have changed. The millions of people on Google, Twitter and Facebook might not see your ad on TV, hear it on the radio or see it in the newspaper. The balloons? Well, perhaps if they drive by your lot they might point them out to their kids.

Today, more than ever, customers drive the marketplace. You can either embrace change and move ahead or get left behind. Customers are in charge and they can make you a hero or a zero quickly. The social media landscape is littered with companies that ignored consumers—they paid for it dearly.

So, how can you reach and retain customers? Let's look at some key social media platforms.

AN INTRODUCTION TO SOCIAL MEDIA CHANNELS

There are thousands of social media channels out there. Here, we will only focus on the top social media outlets relevant to the automotive industry. The technological revolution has enabled easy-access gateways to social media on many devices; smartphones, tablets and laptops are just a few of the many social media friendly devices in the market today. For simplicity's sake, this book will focus on how desktop computers can be utilized in the social media landscape.

In the introduction, we explained why social media is important. The next step is identifying the big players in the world of social media. In this section, we will cover the role and importance of top social media outlets. The platforms in this book are chosen based on their success. Success, in the social media sphere, is determined by the number of users of the social media tool (platform) and the extent to which the tool can keep the users engaged. We strongly believe that both of these factors are essential to ensure success of anything digital.

MEDIA PLATFORMS

Don't be confused when we say social media platform, tool, outlet, service or channel. We use these terms interchangeably. If it helps, just remember that whenever we refer to social media platforms or channels, we are referring to things like Facebook or Twitter.

We want you to be familiar with the major social media outlets before you create accounts and start using them. Here we have compiled a list, with brief descriptions, of social media outlets that we will address in this book.

Twitter

Twitter is a social media service that allows users to share information in short bursts of 140 characters. These short bursts are called "tweets." Tweets are not limited to texts. Users can tweet pictures and links to external Web pages. A "retweet" occurs when a user shares another user's tweet in his or her Twitter page.

Twitter users follow other users and are followed by other users who decide to follow them. The users can decide whom to follow and who can follow them. Companies often use Twitter promotions and contests to increase the number of followers. The idea is to expand your reach by increasing the number of followers.

Recently, Budweiser ran a Twitter campaign asking their followers to help them name a newborn colt. Followers of the Budweiser Twitter page retweeted the original message (tweet), which attracted new followers who wanted to suggest names or wanted to follow the names that other users suggested. The campaign created such a buzz that it attracted the news media. News media attention helped the campaign grow even more. The company successfully acquired thousands of followers to its Twitter page without ever promoting a product or a sale. They just asked for a little help naming a horse and away it went!

With more than 500 million accounts (and growing, and growing, and growing), Twitter leads the pack when it comes to news dissemination. Some say that Twitter has a lower reach (by certain standards), but its capability to form large webs of connections and its ease of use puts Twitter at the very top of our list. It's user-friendly features and the attractive design makes it an agile social media tool. Twitter is one of the easiest ways to broadcast messages.

Facebook

Arguably the top platform in terms of social engagement and based on sheer number of users, Facebook is powerful, but less user friendly. With more than one billion users (and growing, and growing, and growing), 70 percent of Facebook's traffic comes from outside the USA. Facebook's world reach is impossible to ignore. Facebook posts do not show on Google search results pages. Yet, an established Facebook presence is a must-have. We'll say it again, one billion users.

Facebook users are given a page through which they can share various information. As a Facebook user, you add "friends" to your network. When you add something to your Facebook page, it is called a post. Your Facebook friends can "Like" things you post on your page, comment on things you post and share things you post with their friends. As a business, you can add "Likes" from customers, prospects and other interested parties. These "Likes" (here, "Likes" are other Facebook users that hit the Like button on your Facebook business page) can comment on your Facebook posts or share them with their friends. All your posts, as well as the posts from other users that you "friend" or Like, are gathered in a scrolling flow of information called the "News Feed."

Facebook also gives you the ability to place ads. We won't get into Facebook ads in great detail here, but one thing we like about Facebook is that it allows you to drill deep into demographics, hobbies, geography and other important information that helps you to deliver highly targeted information to audiences.

If you strip away the somewhat narcissistic use of Facebook, you will see that it is the world's largest referral network. Facebook users share the good, the bad and the ugly! But in between sharing meatloaf recipes, funny cartoons and "look at me" pictures, Facebook users also spend a lot of time browsing through their News Feed and disseminating tons of information across the globe.

Google+

We are not going to talk a lot about digital politics, but we can tell you that Google and Facebook are competitors. So, after Facebook announced that Bing would be the default search engine within Facebook, Google launched Google+… its own social network!

Google+ consolidates several tools such as Google search, maps and Gmail into one platform. Anyone can set up an individual Google+ page. Businesses can set up (we highly recommend it) or claim a Google+ page for their business.

Google+ is easy to set up and configure. After creating a personal Google+ page at Google.com, users can create additional pages for their businesses, brands, hobbies, etc. and join existing groups of like-minded people to communicate, have video "hang outs," or say positive/negative things about your dealership.

This new social media outlet is an all-in-one tool completely integrated with all of Google's exclusive products. It's a fast-growing, 540-million monthly active user account tool that boasts a large scale world reach and usability. Also, Google+ posts shows up on the Google search engine. So, it is a good idea to include a link to your main website in your Google+ page. This is another must-have social media platform for dealers!

YouTube

YouTube, the No. 1 video outlet in the world, has been uploading videos every day for the last nine years. This Google product also has 70 per-

20

cent of its traffic coming from outside the U.S. It has a live version, great variety and is easy to use. It's well integrated with other social platforms, and is a must-have social media outlet.

For your business, YouTube is a great place to share videos of happy buyers, test drives of the latest car models, and a wide array of reviews and testimonials. Since Google owns YouTube, it loves it! So, naturally, YouTube videos get a considerable boost in search engine results.

Your videos do not have to be high quality. In fact, most of the videos that go "viral" on YouTube have been shot on a smartphone or a basic camcorder.

LinkedIn

LinkedIn is the leading social channel for business. It has a strong presence of more than 170 million users. The interface is focused on networking and is extremely useful. It's mainly used by individuals, but companies have found their way to the platform via ads, groups and human resource profiling.

LinkedIn can produce some search results. You can also use it as a talent recruitment tool. If you are using LinkedIn to promote your dealership, stick with your higher-end models since most LinkedIn users are white-collar professionals.

Myspace

With 44 million users, Myspace is an American social media tool especially useful for musicians to share music. It has good usability, but has a narrow audience. It's free and is a favorite of millennials. So, you can't go wrong by setting up a Myspace account. Try to keep things interesting with minimum effort.

Delicious

This is a great place to store, share and discover Web bookmarks. If you have ever had any Web presence and have posted something catchy, someone most likely added your content to Delicious. If you are not there at all, your content may be under-performing in the social space. Delicious is a good place to measure how your content is being viewed by the general public.

Flickr

This tool is mainly a UK and U.S. image depository. Boasting more than 51 million accounts, Flickr is a good place to promote your photos and reach onlookers. But its lack of features and limited reach makes it not as important as other outlets. Give it a quick browse and decide if it is right for you.

Digg

Digg is a social news website where users can vote stories up or down. It's a great place to test your content and share what you like. Think of it as a community-driven voting booth. At this point you may be thinking, "Isn't all social media the same thing?" Perhaps, but Digg is unique in that it gives every piece of content an equal shot at being the next big thing.

Wikipedia

This is another must-have. An open-source encyclopedia, it's the social media equivalent of your "About Us" page. This is where people will go to learn about you. As of right now, Wikipedia is the fifth most visited website on the Internet. What's remarkable about Wikipedia is that all of its content is written in collaboration with Internet volunteers; anyone with Internet access can write or edit content. In some cases, editing is limited to prevent vandalism or disruptive behavior.

Yelp

Yelp is the online version of the Better Business Bureau. Your customers may go to Yelp to rate your service. The downside is that Yelp gives negative reviews more weight than positive ones; placing negative reviews higher up in your review results.

Most likely, Yelp already has information and reviews about you, but you must actively manage your reviews and recommendations with an appropriate level of customer-relationship management. Given the large community of outspoken and active community locals, you can't afford to ignore Yelp.

FourSquare

With more than 40 million registered users, FourSquare allows people to share their location with friends by "checking in" at various places like restaurants, businesses, events, etc. It has more than 375 million check-ins per year! When users check in at various places, they receive "badges" and titles like "mayor" from Foursquare. So, when someone is busy typing on their smartphone while at your dealership, it could be that they are checking in and telling their friends how ready they are to buy their new ride from you.

WordPress

WordPress is the combination of a website design tool and a community. Many of the websites you visit are set up on the WordPress platform. WordPress can be extremely helpful for your business. The WordPress blog platform is visually appealing and full of features such as add-ons (called plugins) and widgets. It has more than 51 million users.

With high-end usability, WordPress continues to grow, thanks to loyal followers and developers. If you are considering building or rebuilding your website, WordPress is a great option to consider. The flexibility and professional appearance of WordPress comes at a lower price than setting up a regular website. You can also use WordPress to create a site apart from your main website, to which you can add articles and inventory descriptions on-the-fly, without disrupting your main website.

Google loves WordPress. WordPress has plugins that allow you to add an article, then have it automatically added to your other social media channels, e.g. Twitter and Facebook.

Blogger

The second biggest blog platform available is yet another Google product. By now, you probably have started to notice how influential Google is in the social media world; Google's strategy is to provide a one-stop shop, with single sign-in and great reliability. As it is with most blogging platforms, Blogger provides step-by-step guidelines that will help you set up your blog in no time.

Blogengine.net

Blogengine.net will host your blog for a low monthly fee. It boasts ease-of-use and customization. We encourage you to visit blogengine.net and see if this platform suits your needs.

There are more than 1,000 other generic social media outlets that you may learn about and come across as you explore. In the automotive space, there are some social media outlets that are dedicated to automobiles. They are:

CarDomain
The largest social networking site for auto enthusiasts has more than two million users and features 650,000 custom ride profiles. CarDomain also features the "StreetFire" video network and the automotive enthusiast blog "autoholics." Despite its rich features, we do not suggest that you ignore Facebook and YouTube to solely focus on CarDomain; rather, we encourage you to add CarDomain as an addition to your social media landscape.

RSS Feed
Although this is not a social media channel, we feel it is relevant and important because it enables content aggregation. RSS stands for Really Simple Syndication and it is a way to share content you create without requiring a user to visit your website. WHAT? Why would anyone want that? Imagine this: You have an inventory of cars that is constantly changing. If I (the user) can see your inventory on my Google+ or my Yahoo! homepage, I will be familiar with your brand, and when it is time to buy a car, I will most likely give you a try.

HANDY TOOLS

Free SocialMention • HowSociable • Grader.com • TweetStats

Paid Radian6 • Sysomos • Social Radar • NetBase

Beginner
Before you begin, let's talk about a few ground rules. The only bad press you get in social media is press that you don't respond to. Unhappy customers will most likely post something negative on your social media channels. When this happens, your response to the customer will be key to how you are viewed in the social media world. If you made a mistake, admit it and fix it. If you think the posting is from a competitor, suggest that the posting party contact you directly to resolve their problem. If they don't contact you in a couple of weeks, note that in your response to their post and encourage them to respond.

Also, in the Internet world, it is ok to use someone else's content as long as you give them credit. But, as a rule, don't steal content. It's not cool and it's usually illegal.

Finally, understand that social media strategies may take time to show results. Social media is a lot like getting married. You start with dating, then move to courtship, then to marriage. These steps take time. Be patient. You shouldn't be spending a ton of money on your social media campaign. So relax, have fun and let your social media success develop into business success.

SET UP A GMAIL ACCOUNT

Set up a Gmail account (Fig 1.1). If you haven't done anything yet, this is the perfect way to scratch the surface.

FIGURE 1.1

You're going to need a Gmail account for Google+ and YouTube, so you might as well set one up now.

Open an Internet browser and type in "Gmail.com," and it will take you to the Gmail homepage. Set up is simple; just follow the steps. Gmail will send a confirming email to whatever other email address you give during set up. As soon as you click on the confirmation link sent to that email, your Gmail account will be active.

CREATING YOUR SOCIAL MEDIA CHANNELS

Facebook

Go to www.facebook.com using an Internet browser (Firefox, Google Chrome, Internet Explorer, Safari, etc.). Note: Since Facebook is Web-based, you can access your account from anywhere with any computer/smartphone at any time; as long as you have Internet access.

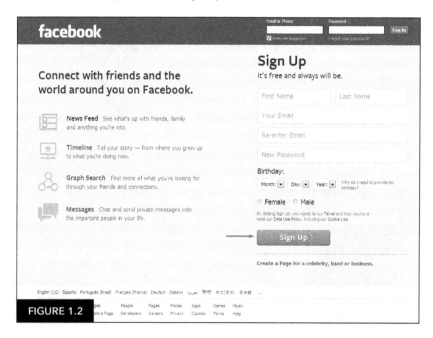

FIGURE 1.2

You will need to set up a personal Facebook profile before you can add a business page (Fig 1.2). Facebook also requires that your profile have at least 25 "Likes," before you are allowed to set up a business page. This is Facebook's way of confirming that you are a real person who actually knows other real people. Twenty-five might sound like a lot, but once you add your significant other, kids, colleagues and employees, getting 25 Likes will be a breeze. These business pages or "fan pages" as some call it, can have unlimited followers and are typically used to promote brands and companies.

FIGURE 1.3

How to post text, image and video

Adding content to your dealership's Facebook page is quick and easy. To create a new post, click in the "What have you been up to, _____" text box at the top of your Facebook page (Fig 1.3). Type what you want to post in the box and click "Post." The item will immediately appear on your Facebook "wall" for all to see. That said, you may want to cut and paste what you want to post into a Word or text document first for spell-checking purposes.

To post an image or video, click on the "Photo/Video" icon on top of the Status box. You can then click Attach Photo/Video and choose the file you want to upload or click on "Create Photo Album" to make a folder to hold photos (Fig 1.4). The folder can be given a specific label, such as "New Cars Just Arrived." Once your image is uploaded, you can click in the "Say something about this" text box and write a comment, e.g. "Check out this low-mileage 2012 Honda Accord that just arrived. It's fully loaded!" Then click "Post" and your image, as well as any text that you typed, will appear on your Facebook wall.

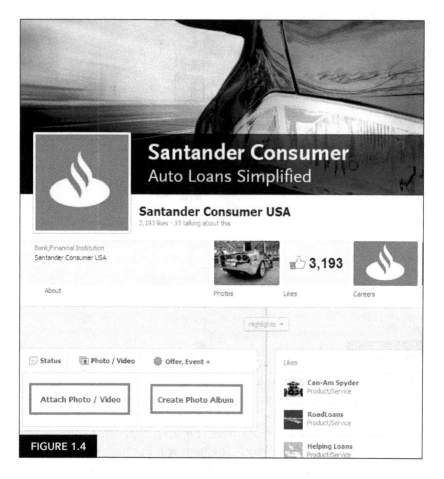

FIGURE 1.4

How to "Like" others:

Facebook uses the term "Like" to refer to things that you like or recommend. When you Like something, it will show up in your scrollbar in the upper-right corner. With the Like feature, you don't leave a comment. You can also Unlike something that you Liked. Liking something also refers to Liking a Page. Say there is a particular automobile manufacturer you want to help promote; you can go to the company's Facebook page and Like it. Then, whenever the Page/company you Like has content updates, the content will appear on your Facebook Home News Feed. Likes from your Friends will appear on the upper right corner of your Facebook page and things that you Like will appear on your friends' pages as you Like them (Fig 1.5).

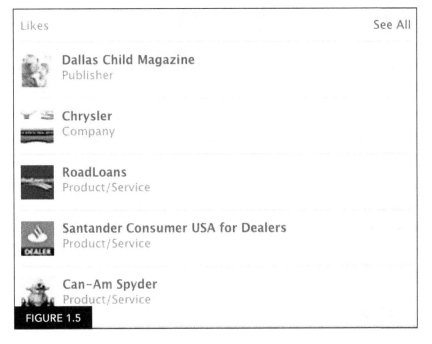

Likes   See All

Dallas Child Magazine
Publisher

Chrysler
Company

RoadLoans
Product/Service

Santander Consumer USA for Dealers
Product/Service

Can–Am Spyder
Product/Service

FIGURE 1.5

How to get others to "Like" you

You want to get as many people as possible to Like your page. Social media is, after all, SOCIAL. The more popular your site is, the more potential car buyers it will attract. Make sure to promote your Facebook page on all your printed materials: business cards, dealer signage, license plate borders, etc. You can spread the word via word-of-mouth. Any time you mention the fact that you have a Facebook page to someone—on the phone, in person, via e-mail or text message—there is potential for building Likes and customers.

You can send out an email to your email contacts and invite them to Like you and connect with you on Facebook.

- Run a contest. It's simple. It also rewards your followers. The return on investment can be measured by the number of participants and the number of new Likes that are added to your page. Here's an example: Most dealerships have promotional material—T-shirts, koozies, mugs, pens, notepads, etc. Pick an item and promote it for a giveaway for people that Like you on Facebook. Anyone that comes to your lot or calls the dealership to inquire about inventory is a potential Facebook friend. You don't have to spend a lot of money on promotional

items. Ten personalized mugs can cost as little as $3 each, but can give your Facebook page positive traction with Likes and comments.
- This is also an opportunity to think outside the box. Think of something creative, yet relevant to your dealership.
- Take springtime: Host a spring automobile sale at your dealership and give away items associated with spring. Post the items on your Facebook page. When people come to your lot, hand out "mystery boxes" filled with a chance to win promotional items. It's simple, but it can make a huge difference in building a Facebook following and adding Likes. Always remember to have fun when you promote.

The key to Facebook success is to consistently communicate interesting, funny, compelling and attractive content. Here are some examples:

Fun and compelling
"Help us give this poor car a proper burial! Stop by the dealership this week and write whatever you want on this car before it goes to the crusher. We'll donate $1 for every signature on the car to the local animal shelter and we'll post video of the car being crushed next week."

Political without being political
"If the Republican candidate wins the upcoming election, all of our red cars will be $1,000 off until such and such a date. If the Democrat wins, all our blue cars are $1,000 off."

Tugs at the heartstrings
"The local animal shelter just brought us our new dealership dog and we need help naming him. The winner gets a $50 gift certificate to (one of your business owner customer's business)."

In each of these examples, you can specifically mention the candidate, the animal shelter and brand with a "tag." These tags will help your post get picked up on other people's news feeds; you might also get some press if it gets noticed by a reporter. A simple way to tag is to add the # sign, e.g. #animalshelter. You can arbitrarily create tags based on the content of your post.

How often you add content to your dealership's Facebook page is totally up to you, but we suggest that you post something at least once a day.

Twitter

To set up a Twitter account for your dealership, visit www.twitter.com (Fig 1.6). Come up with a username that is easy to remember and promote. For example, if you dealership is M&M Car Sales, pick a username like @mmcarsales or @mm_carsales (Fig 1.7). You will get a confirmation email and your Twitter account will be active as soon as you click on the confirmation link.

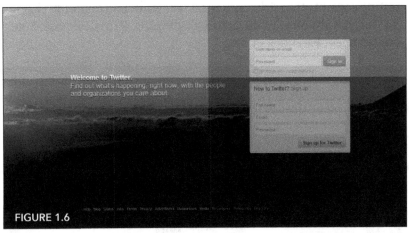

FIGURE 1.6

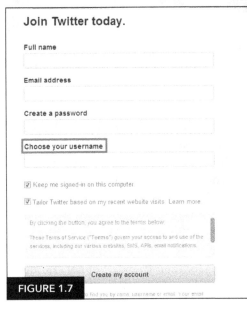

FIGURE 1.7

Twitter Names

All Twitter usernames begin with @. Additional note: Since Twitter only allows for 140 characters, a shorter Twitter name works best, so others wanting to (and we hope they do) retweet your tweets can add their own message to your tweet — this is social media at its core.

The next step is to find people or brands that you want to follow. These might be your car brands, car magazines, car clubs, etc. Often, when you follow someone, they will follow you back. This is a common Twitter courtesy that does not extend to companies. But, you can still leverage this courtesy as you add Twitter followers who are also customers.

How do you post text, image and video?

Twitter is probably the easiest social media platform when it comes to creating content. The trick is fitting all you want to say into 140 characters. You can always tweet links to a longer piece if they are posted on your Google+, Facebook or blog.

FIGURE 1.8

Once your account is set up, click on the blue "feather pen" icon in the upper-right corner of your Twitter page to post a new tweet. (Fig 1.8) A text box with the heading "What's happening?" will appear. Click inside the box and start composing your tweet. Your available character count will be automatically counted in the bottom right corner next to the Tweet button. If you see a negative number that means you have exceeded the allotted 140 character count. As we suggested earlier, you may want to cut and paste what you want to post into a Word or text document first and check for spelling errors. Twitter does not have an autocorrect feature and tweet errors are common, which is fine for individuals who are tweeting for their friends, but not OK for an automobile business that wants to look professional at all times.

If you are within the character count and have written all you want to say, your tweet is ready to be posted. Unless you want to add a link or a photo. To add a photo, click on the icon that looks like a camera on the lower left hand corner of the textbox and select the desired image from your computer. To add a link, simply copy the link and paste it in the text box. To post your tweet, click on the "Tweet" button when you are ready (Fig 1.9).

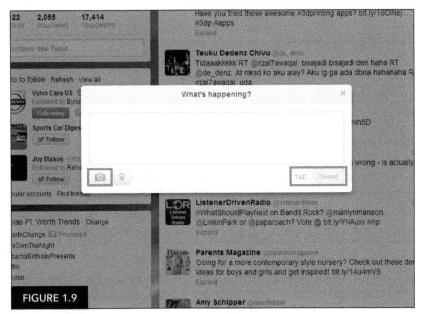

FIGURE 1.9

Congratulations! Your tweet has now been posted and all of your followers will see it on their Twitter feed.

How often you should tweet depends on what you have going on. If you feel you have something relevant to say, then tweet away. Here is an example: "The first person to test drive the new Ram Truck gets two free tickets to a major league baseball game. #mmcarsales" Notice the hashtag (#) included at the end. Twitter users place hashtags before relevant keywords (for a dealer, it would be the dealership name) to frequently appear on a Twitter search. If someone clicks on a hashtagged word in a tweet, the click will bring up all tweets relevant to that tag. There is no rule for the optimum number of tweets per day.

Studies suggest that posting a minimum of one and maximum of 20 posts per day is ideal. Somewhere in between one and 20 is probably a good place to be. These posts should include retweets (that is, re-posting a tweet you like and think others who follow your dealer account would find relevant), promotional content, positive reviews of automobiles you sell, pictures of vehicles on your lot (with descriptions) and other relevant, non-self-promotional content.

TIME TO TWEET

Spread out your tweets throughout the day. It's better not to post a bunch of content at the same time or several posts within seconds of each other.

How to sync with Facebook

Your tweets can also be automatically posted to Facebook. To sync the two profiles, click on the icon next to the feather pen and select "Settings" from the drop down menu (Fig 1.10). Then click on "Profile" and select the box that says "Connect to Facebook" (Fig 1.11). Click on that button and any tweet that you post from then on will be posted on your Facebook page.

FIGURE 1.10

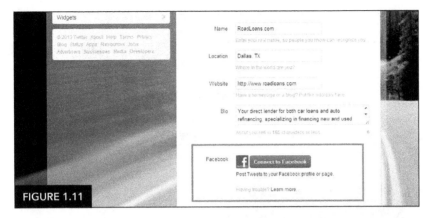

FIGURE 1.11

We do not recommend syncing the two accounts. Here's why: 1. Your audiences may differ from one social media channel to another. 2. You should not just create noise. Rather, you should focus on adding value. People often unlike or unfollow companies that are too noisy. Focus on the quality of your content rather than the quantity.

How to follow others

To follow someone on Twitter, locate the person or business you want to follow and click on the "Follow" button. You will then be following that account. As a dealer, it's a good idea to follow Twitter accounts that are relevant to your business. Kelley Blue Book (@KelleyBlueBook), Car and Driver (@CARandDRIVER), Cars.com (@carsdotcom), Consumer Guide Auto (@cgautomotive), Automotive News (@Automotive_News), and many others are great to connect with. And of course, depending on the vehicles and models you are involved with, it's always good to follow all of those accounts. Again, the more in the mix you are, the more followers you'll attract to your account.

How to grow your Twitter followers

Like Facebook, your Twitter account and the Twitter logo should be anywhere and everywhere you are—on your letterhead, on the doors to your dealership, on your business cards, mentioned in the outgoing phone message. To be successful in acquiring more followers, you need to let everyone know that you are on Facebook and Twitter. When you meet someone, mention that you have Facebook and Twitter accounts, and that your dealership frequently announces promotions, sales and new arrivals through these channels.

LinkedIn

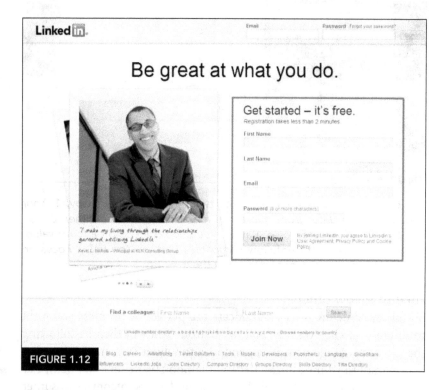

FIGURE 1.12

How to set up an account

To set up a LinkedIn account, open an Internet browser and visit www. linkedin.com (Fig 1.12). Create your dealership's profile by filling out a brief description in the overview. Include where you are located. Be sure to include links to your company's website as well as to your Google+, Facebook and Twitter accounts. You can include as little or as much information as you want. Also, add a Google map so that customers can find your dealership if they see you on LinkedIn.

If you're hiring, you can post job openings on LinkedIn so that potential candidates can contact you directly to inquire about the positions. It's best to assign a point person who has a LinkedIn profile to manage your dealer LinkedIn page. That way, job candidates have a point of contact if they have questions.

Adding content to your LinkedIn profile is similar to updating your Facebook status. The only real difference is navigating around the site.

How to connect with others

The basic purpose of LinkedIn is to connect with others in a business professional setting. The auto industry has a lot of ways to connect with like-minded businesses and individuals. You can start by sending invites to people you know and other dealers, customers, etc. "Discussions" like "New and Used Car Sales," "Smart Repair Body Shops," "Top Workplaces," "Remarketing Tools," and "Q&As with Industry Experts" are examples of how you can start conversations that are relevant to the industry, and how trends affect your dealership.

You can sync your other social media profiles with LinkedIn, so when you post something on Twitter or Facebook, it will appear in your LinkedIn page as well. Once everything is synced properly, the content that you post on any of the synced profiles will show on the home feed of your LinkedIn connections. However, we do not recommend that you do this because your LinkedIn profile should be more professional than your other social media channels.

CONNECT WITH YOUR INDUSTRY

A great way to connect via LinkedIn is through Groups and Associations. Groups like Digital Car Dealers, Automotive Management Professionals, Automotive Internet Marketing, Automotive Industry Professionals Worldwide, and others will connect you with automotive peers and keep you up-to-date on all auto-industry related topics.

J.P.Morgan

Asset Management

Asset Management provides institutional, high-net-worth and individual investor clients with high quality global investment management in equities, fixed income, real assets, hedge funds, private equity and cash liquidity. By building a reputation for investment excellence and superior service,...

Recommend · Share

31 recommendations

J.P.Morgan

Corporate and Investment Bank

J.P. Morgan's Corporate & Investment Bank is a global leader across banking, markets and investor services. The world's most important corporations, governments and institutions entrust us with their business in more than 100 countries. The Corporate & Investment Bank provides strategic advice,...

Recommend · Share

16 recommendations

Google+

FIGURE 1.13

Setting up a Google+ account is easy and free. You need a Gmail account to claim your Google+ page. Simply log in to your Gmail account and click on the "You+" button located at the upper left side of the screen and follow the steps to create your page. After that, create a "Brand Page;" this will be your dealership's Google+ page (Fig 1.13).

Within the Google+ setup page, be sure to add your address, photos of your building, vehicles and staff, a link to your company website and your phone number. You can also add a few categories for your business type. All these little things will make you more search-engine friendly. Your Google+ page should be viewed as a website. Make sure that all the information is complete and accurate; this will help you attract more potential customers.

You can log back into your Google+ page whenever you need to change or add information.

Blogs

Blog is short for "Web log." Blogs are becoming increasingly popular, for example, as a way for people and businesses to express their individual style and voice. Dealerships can use blogs to write customer-oriented articles addressing issues that customers may encounter during their car search. There are many great blogs in the auto industry: MSN Autos, Cars.com and Edmunds are just a few examples. These blogs may give you an idea about what you can do with your blog. Do your own research on how these are written and how effective you think they are. Figure out what you like and don't like about these blogs and keep a pros and cons sheet for each blog. That way you will be able to see the content choices of others in the industry. Also, it may inspire you to do something new and unique with your own.

The top three blog engines are WordPress, Blogger, and Typepad. Let's focus on Blogger.

How to set up an account

To create a blog for your dealership, log onto Blogger.com using your Gmail account username and password. Blogger is a Google product, so you can also access Blogger after logging in to your Gmail and clicking the "more" button and choosing "Blogger."

Blogger.com has a user-friendly interface that makes it easy to create a blog. Be sure to have a digital copy of your dealership logo handy so you can use it for the blog.

Meet with your sales team and employees to brainstorm ideas for your dealership's blog. Find out if your employees are interested in submitting stories for the blog. Regardless of how many contributors you have for your blog, it's best to have a point person who handles the traffic flow of the content. This person will know the Blogger password and will do all the posting. They will also control the blog's tone and message. This will ensure consistency and filter negative or unauthorized use of the blog.

You can also subscribe to other blogs. Seek out blogs that are relevant to the auto business. Sites such as MSN Autos, Cars.com and Edmunds do a great job at covering industry-related topics and posting engaging content. It's also good to subscribe to blogs from the makes and models that you handle. Some of these companies have blogs and some don't. Regardless, publications like *Car & Driver*, *Motor Trend*, *Road & Track* and even *USA Today* and the *New York Times* have blogs run by their staff. These blogs can keep you in the loop on what's happening in the industry. You can also add their blog content to your Facebook, Twitter and blog so that you don't have to constantly create new content.

How to get others to subscribe to your blog

To get others to subscribe to your blog, you have to get the word out that you have a blog. If people don't know that you have a blog, they can't subscribe. Right? So, make sure your blog is mentioned in all of your media material.

Yelp

Yelp allows you to promote your business and receive reviews about your products and services from its users.

Like Google+, Yelp will most likely have a page set up for your business that could be claimed like your Google+ page.

First, you need to set up a personal Yelp account. Go to Yelp.com and follow the set-up procedures (Fig 1.14). By now, you will notice that the sign-up process for most social media channels is similar.

Once you confirm your personal Yelp account, you can claim your business account, which will allow you to add photos, your logo and written content about your dealership. Claiming your page allows you to respond to all reviews that are posted by other Yelp users, so this is an important platform to have. Once again, promote your Yelp page in all media material.

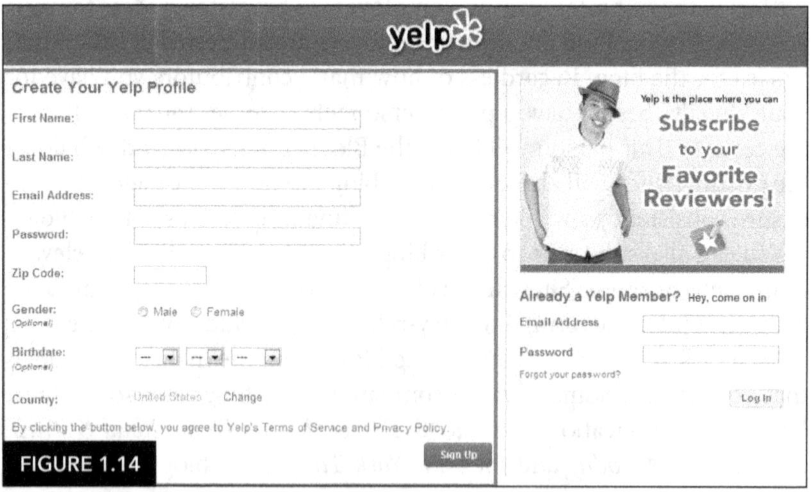

FIGURE 1.14

QR Codes

Here is a QR Code we created for the Santander Consumer USA Facebook page for dealers. QR stands for "Quick Response" and code represents the image composition. A QR Code acts as a link between printed material and digital content. You've probably seen QR Codes on products, movie posters, menus and other sources. They look like a square filled with lines, dashes and dots. You need a QR Reader to read a QR Code. Generally, QR Readers are free and work on most mobile phones and other mobile devices that have a camera. For example, if you were reading a short newspaper ad and the information interested you, you can point your Reader to the QR Code and voilà! Your phone browser takes you to additional information.

FREE QR READERS

Grab a free QR code reader from your mobile phone's App Store.

If you point a QR Reader to the QR Code on page 41, it will take you to the Santander Dealer Facebook page. If you have a smartphone, get a QR Reader from your Android Market or App Store. Google Shopper is a great QR Code app, because it allows you to read any QR Code out there. And yes, there are different types of codes.

QR Codes can help shorten the material you give to prospects. If they are interested in learning more about a particular vehicle, the QR Code can direct them to additional information. For example, if you are running a newspaper ad or article about a year-end sale, you can use a QR Code that will link the ad to your inventory Web page. When someone uses your QR Code, it shows that they are interested in what you have to offer.

QR Codes can also be used for Web addresses, email addresses, phone numbers, to send text messages, business cards and schedule events!

YouTube

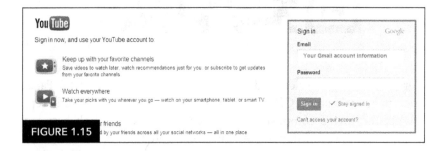

FIGURE 1.15

Signing up for a YouTube account is easy. You can log in using your Gmail account (Fig 1.15). Once you confirm your account, it will create a "channel." One account can have multiple channels, but not the other way around. You may want to consider this if you manage multiple brands.

GOOGLE BAR NAVIGATION

Once you log into your Gmail account, the black Google bar enables you to access your Gmail, Google+, YouTube, Picasa, Blogger and many other Google applications available to you. This is why we encouraged you to create a Gmail account at the very beginning of this book.

ROOKIE TO-DO LIST

Now that you've set up your accounts, let's go over some next steps.

1 Think about your overall marketing plan; don't overthink it. Try to keep it as simple as possible, and it will help you deliver your messages clearly and consistently. You can always expand your plan later, but when you are starting out, it's better to take your time and examine how you want to use social media in the "big picture." Again, you can always expand or tweak your marketing plan as you get more accustomed to how social media works in your business.

2 Take one week to just jot down notes for your "big picture" marketing plan. Revisit your notes during a quiet time.

3 Establish your marketing goals. Like all successful endeavors, it's best to have a plan. Sounds simple right? But, you'd be surprised by the number of people who just jump right in and start working without having a plan. They realize that they forgot something after getting deep into a project and end up going backward; often to the very beginning. This is not only counterproductive, but also frustrating. All this can be avoided by establishing your marketing goals right from the start. Ask yourself these questions: "What do I hope to accomplish with social media?" "Who needs to be involved in the process and in what capacity?" "What will be my overall (and CONSISTENT) message?" "What sort of timeline am I looking at to accomplish these goals?"

4 Make sure that every one of your goals for social media is measurable in real data. For example, "I want to add 25 new Facebook Likes in the first 45 days of launching my Facebook page," or "I want 50 people to show up at the dealership and autograph that junk car for charity this week." If you can't clearly measure it with actual data, it's not a goal.

Answer Questions #5 - #10

5 Who is my audience? A simple question, but it must be answered before developing a social media plan. Think about who you want to reach (and be social with) and build a generic personal profile

with general characteristics of your audience. Zero-in on details of the person when creating the profile; give them a name (even if it's John Doe), define the age range, define spending habits, etc. In other words, take general characteristics of your customers and create a generic customer profile. After you have established who your audience is, it's easier to create targeted social media content. Getting your audience to engage with your content is extremely crucial in social media, so think about content that will keep them coming back to your social media outlets.

6 How do I reach them? Think about which outlets will work best for your audience. Are they social-media savvy? If so, what types of social media do they use the most (Facebook, Twitter, YouTube, etc.)? How did you reach the most-recent person who bought a car from you? Start there. Then, think about what you can do to reach their friends through social media.

7 What problems can I help them solve? The automobile business isn't rocket science, but that doesn't mean that purchasing a vehicle is not complicated. It's good to know what general problems your customers have. How can you, as their dealer, solve these problems? More important, how can you use social media to address these problems? If they have problems, you should have answers ... it's your job as the dealer.

8 What are the most recurring questions you get from customers? Maybe they center around financing. If so, create a hypothetical example that will answer those questions in a way that makes sense to the average customer.

9 How much am I willing to spend to reach my prospects? Although most of the tools we have outlined in this section are free to set up, there are still budget-related considerations that you should address. Cost of discounts, promotions, gifts, etc. need to be taken to account when creating your social media marketing plan. Also, using professionals to handle any or all of these functions has a cost; your time has a cost! Determining how much money you want to allocate to social media is essential. We suggest that you determine a monthly budget amount and monitor your results in the various social media outlets over time. Adjust your efforts based on those results.

10 How can I entertain and inform? When creating content for social media, keep in mind that the purpose of your content is to facilitate dialogue. You should build a relationship with your customers, so approach your content with that mindset. What do you think your customers enjoy reading about? What movies and songs are popular? Sit back and think about how you can use your content to both inform and entertain.

11 Take an hour to surf Facebook. Look at different ads, news feeds, pages, etc. Pay attention to how people and businesses interact. Notice the good, the bad and the ugly! Emulate the good, avoid the bad. Simple.

12 Gather your staff and ask them for 10 outrageous promotion, contest or sales ideas that you can implement in the next six months. You may be shocked at how good the suggestions are once you let them know that these ideas are for your social media channels.

13 Ask your staff for 10 subject ideas that they think your customers and prospects are interested in. For an example "best car safety seats" is a subject idea.

14 Create an exit-interview form that your salesmen/women can hand out to prospects that DON'T buy. This will help you gather valuable information while sending a positive message to the prospect—that you really care about doing business with them.

15 Ask all of your staff to like your Facebook page, follow your Twitter page and give you positive reviews on Google+ and Yelp from their personal accounts. The reality is that competitors and site owners like Yelp may work against you, so there's nothing inappropriate about an employee saying that they, "loved their experience" with your dealership.

No one knows what's relevant to your customers better than your customers themselves, so don't be afraid to ask what they would like to read about. Maybe it's the newest gadget that's being added to a car. Or, a comparison of sound systems of on few models on your lot. Maybe a side-by-side comparison of 0-60 for a few cars at your dealership. If you were buying a car, what would you like to read about? You can also use other industry-related material like magazine articles, blog posts, YouTube videos, etc.

16 What content will compel them to purchase what you have to offer? This is the $25,000 question. To answer this question, you have to focus on what makes your dealership unique. Maybe your customer service is consistently ranked in the top tier. Maybe you are the largest dealer of a particular make and model in your area. Perhaps you have unique offers that other dealers don't have. Whatever the case, make yourself stand out and get the attention of customers. Once you draw the customers to your dealership and they get a great deal, they will spread the word and surprise! You get more business. Anyone not interested in selling more cars?

17 Create a place on the homepage of your website for your social media icons. Most websites have icons for Facebook, Twitter, YouTube, etc., on their homepage. Usually, these icons are on the upper right corner or in a "Connect With Us" section in the bottom right of the homepage. These icons are linked directly to their social media pages.

18 Find things to give away for free; this will bring customers to your site. It may be as simple as a free carwash.

19 Give some personality to your site. Have fun with your site and get creative. Include images and text that reflect your overall approach to business. Use photos that show excitement and joy. Don't use stock photos! You don't have to be a professional photographer to snap great pictures for your social media sites. Be sure the images you post are exciting, relevant and original. Say you just got a new shipment of vehicles; take a picture of the delivery. Take a picture of the truck pulling in to your lot with the shipment still on its trailer.

20 Take a picture of your next buyer. Add the buyer picture to your Facebook page.

21 Add the buyer picture to your Google+ page. Add the buyer picture to your website.

22 Shoot a simple video testimonial from your next five happy customers.

23 Transcribe the buyer's testimonial into written form.

24 Load the video to your YouTube channel.

25 Add the transcribed testimonial to your Facebook page. Tweet a link to your transcribed testimonial; include your website address in the tweet.

26 Give your new buyer a gift certificate for a local restaurant after they give you a great review on Google+ and Yelp.

27 Include lots of details on pages about your products. Include: testimonials, photos, concepts and how the products solve buyers' problems. Again, your best supporters are your customers! Satisfied and returning customers are ideal testimonial candidates for your dealership.

28 Consider using easy-to-use blogging software like Blogger or WordPress.

29 Create your own blog. Choose a URL for your blog (e.g. yourcompany.com/blog).

30 Name your blog and create a tagline. You can run with your dealership name (Steve's Ford) or think up something creative that sets it apart from the main page of your website (Deals on Wheels).

31 Start commenting on blogs that you find interesting. Make sure that you understand blogging etiquette by reading the blogs first.)

32 Allow readers to leave comments on your blog. Facilitating conversation is great and opinions that are different from yours are OK. Most blog-hosting sites (WordPress, BlogEngine, Posterous), let you turn comments on or off. If the "leave comments" option is turned on, readers can leave comments on your blog posts. Don't forget that you reserve the right to remove inappropriate comments (spam, profanity, etc.).

33 Customize your blog. Use designs, colors, bold headlines… get creative! Some of the best blogs are ones that not only provide good content, but are also visually pleasing.

34 Include your logo and colors. Always, have your brand logo and colors in your main blog page. It helps readers to connect with your brand. If they have already been to your lot and are familiar with your brand, the logo will help them reconnect with their experience with your dealership.

Include links that people can use to find out more about you/your company on a sidebar

35 Write a blog post. Remember to provide valuable information. Add an image that matches your post. Every blog post should give the reader information they can use. No one wants to read a post about something they already know or about something they are not interested in.

36 Mention your blog in your newsletter. Anytime you put out a newsletter (perhaps you do a monthly release), mention that readers can also keep up with information about your dealership through your blog. Give a brief description of your blog and its content.

37 Make plans to add your blog URL to all print material.

38 Add a sticker or stamp with your blog URL to your current printed materials.

39 List your blog with Technorati (a blog indexing site). Technorati manages Web content.

Social Media in One Word

One word that sums up everything you need to know about succeeding in the world of social media is "communication." Social media is about building relationships, connecting with people, making sure your customers know what you have to offer and delivering the best service possible. Did you notice that all of these tasks require communication?

Social media is also organic. In this context, organic means that social media is always changing and growing. How do you keep up with change and growth? Effective communication can reduce confusion and difficulties because good communication involves informing and listening. Social media is a great platform to inform your customers, but don't forget to listen to them. Effective communication goes both ways.

To be successful in social media, you must communicate regularly with your customers. Your posts and tweets should reflect the fact that you are interested in finding out more about your customers' needs–with the ultimate goal of providing excellent service

For example, tweet about a new car you have on the lot and include a link to an article from a reputable publication about the car. Also, mention that you are glad to answer any questions about the car. There are a number of ways you can reach out to your customers. Remember to keep the content relevant. Most important, provide opportunities for your customers to communicate.

SOCIAL MEDIA POLICY TEMPLATE

It is important to have guidelines for your social media use. We highly recommend that you create a social media policy for your dealership. It is always better to be safe than sorry. Having clear policies will prevent confusion and problems in the long run, so do this at the beginning of your venture. This template will give you a general idea of what it should look like:

Your Company Name
Social Media Policy Compliance

BY POSTING ON ANY COMPANY NAME SOCIAL MEDIA SITE YOU AGREE TO THESE TERMS:
Company Name has opened publicly facing pages on social media sites for viewing content and/or videos and posting comments about Company Name and its products and services, hereby referred to as (Abbreviation of Company Name. We will use CN here). These social media sites include but are not limited to various blogs, Facebook, Twitter, YouTube, Google+, bulletin boards, networks, multi-media and news media sites or other user generated content sites ("Social Media Sites"). By accessing, viewing and/or posting any content related directly or indirectly to CN on any Social Media Site on the Internet, you accept, without limitation or qualification, the following terms of use. If you do not agree to the terms of this Policy, you may not view or post any content to any social media site on the Internet, while present at or representing CN. Your use of social media sites is acceptance of this policy and has the same effect as if you had actually physically signed an agreement.

1 As a CN employee you must adhere to this MEDIA AND SOCIAL NETWORKING POLICY. Employees are prohibited from posting any content that is considered Non-public Personal Information (NPI) in nature include financial advice on any social media site. You are also prohibited from using the social media site to provide financial opinions or financial commentary. Posters requesting financial information will be asked to contact the CN customer service department at 888-XXX-XXXX.

2 As a guest posting content to any social media site on the Internet, you agree that you will not: violate any local, state, federal and international laws and regulations, including but not limited to copyright and intellectual property rights laws regarding any content that you send or receive via this policy; transmit any material (by uploading, posting, email or otherwise) that is unlawful, disruptive, threatening, profane, abusive, harassing, embarrassing, tortious, defamatory, obscene, libelous, pornographic or is an invasion of another's privacy, is hateful or racially, ethnically or otherwise objectionable (as solely determined in CN's discretion). Moreover, impersonating any person or entity or falsely stating or otherwise misrepresenting your affiliation with a person or entity is also prohibited. Transmitting any material (by uploading, posting, email or otherwise) that you do not have a right to make available under any law or under contractual or fiduciary relationships is also prohibited. Transmitting any material (by uploading, posting, email or otherwise) that infringes any patent, trademark, trade secret, copyright or other proprietary rights of any party is also prohibited. Transmitting (by uploading, posting, email or otherwise) any unsolicited or unauthorized advertising (including advertising of non-CN services or products), promotional materials, "junk mail," "spam," "chain letters," "pyramid schemes" or any other form of solicitation is also prohibited; transmit any material (by uploading, posting, email or otherwise) that contains software viruses, worms, disabling code, or any other computer code, files or programs designed to interrupt, destroy or limit the functionality of any computer software or hardware or telecommunications equipment is also prohibited. Any harassing of another is also prohibited. Collecting or storing, or attempting to collect or store, personal data about third parties

without their knowledge or consent is also prohibited. Sending confidential personal or financial information NPI is also prohibited.

3 CN reserves the right to monitor, prohibit, restrict, block, suspend, terminate, delete or discontinue your access to any social media site, at any time, without notice and for any reason and in its sole discretion. CN may remove, delete, block, filter or restrict by any other means in CN's sole discretion. You understand and agree that CN may disclose your social media communications and activities both internally and externally in response to lawful requests by governmental authorities, including Patriot Act requests, judicial orders, warrants or subpoenas. You agree that in the event that CN exercises any of its rights for any reason, CN will have no liability to you.

4 Social media participants shall defend, indemnify, and hold CN and its corporate affiliates and their respective officers, directors, employees, contractors, agents, successors and assigns harmless from and against, and shall promptly reimburse them for any and all losses, claims, damages, settlements, costs, and liabilities of any nature whatsoever (including reasonable attorneys' fees) to which any of them may become subject arising out of, based upon, as a result of, or in any way connected with, your posting of any content to a social media site, any third party claims of infringement or any breach of this Policy.

5 YOU EXPRESSLY ACKNOWLEDGE THAT YOU ASSUME ALL RESPONSIBILITY RELATED TO THE SECURITY, PRIVACY, AND CONFIDENTIALITY RISKS INHERENT IN SENDING ANY CONTENT OVER THE INTERNET. By its very nature, a website AND THE INTERNET cannot be absolutely protected against intentional or malicious intrusion attempts. CN does not control the platforms owned by social media sites.

6 CN DOES NOT WARRANT ANY SAFEGUARD AGAINST ANY such interceptions or compromises to your information. When posting any content on an Internet site, you should think carefully about your own privacy in disclosing detailed or private information about yourself and your family. FURTHERMORE, CN DOES NOT ENDORSE ANY PRODUCT, SERVICE, VIEWS OR CONTENT DISPLAYED ON THE SOCIAL MEDIA SITE.

7 THIS POLICY MAY BE UPDATED AT ANY TIME WITHOUT NOTICE, AND EACH TIME A USER ACCESSES A SOCIAL NETWORKING SITE, THE NEW POLICY WILL GOVERN US-AGE EFFECTIVE UPON POSTING. To remain in compliance, CN suggests that you review the Policy, as well as the other website policies, at regular intervals. By continuing to post any content after such new terms are posted, you accept and agree to any and all such modifications to this Policy.

This is just a template. It is your responsibility to consult your legal counsel to ensure that this document addresses the needs and requirements of your organization.

THINGS TO KEEP IN MIND FOR ROOKIES

1 *Don't just sit on the sidelines, get in the game.* As with anything in life, social media requires learning and practice. It's not that difficult to pick up and perfect; evenfor a rookie. The most important thing is to get involved. Start small if you have to. Set up a Twitter account and post a tweet. Just a simple tweet. Use this as an example if you want: "We're having a great sale this weekend at YourName Ford. Come on out and see for yourself. Free food. 100s of vehicles priced to sell." It's that easy. You'll get the hang of it in no time.

2 *Place the Twitter, Facebook, YouTube and Google + icons on your website.* If you don't have your social media icons on your main website, you need to post them immediately. When someone visits your main site, having your social media channels easily accessible makes it easier for them to find you (Fig 1.16). You may have to talk to the person in charge of your website to get this done.

3 *Avoid bothering people with useless information. Your customers are as busy as you are.* So, make sure that your posts, tweets, and other content is relevant and useful to your readers. If you post valuable content, customers will notice and pay attention. Heck, they might even share your content and spread the word.

4 *Don't keep score.* Don't worry about how many Likes, Fans and Followers you have. You can drive yourself crazy by constantly check-

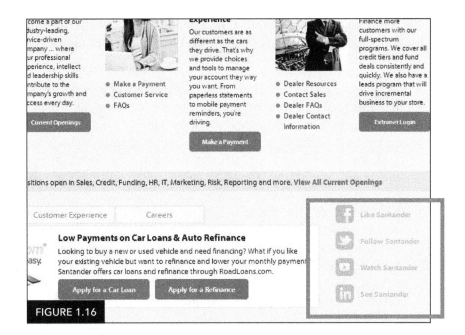

FIGURE 1.16

ing how many Followers, Likes, Fans, etc. that you have or don't have. Just keep posting good content and reach as many people as possible. To paraphrase one of our favorite movies–if you post it, they will come.

5 *Read what others are doing.* Stay educated. The good thing and the bad thing about social media is that there is so much content out there. It's a good idea to create bookmarks for sites with relevant content. You can even create a Word document that has links to relevant social media sites. Keep the document on your desktop. We recommend that you visit these sites in the morning, so you are up-to-date on the latest social media trends.

6 *Explore newer social media platforms.* It's easier to make a name on smaller communities and there are smaller sites that have started to pick up steam! Sites like Pinterest and Instagram are examples of how rapidly new social media platforms can grow. Seek out new channels and get in the game when they are starting out makes it easier to build a presence; it also gives you a chance to ride the waves as they grow.

7 *Follow people in your industry.* The automotive industry has a lot of representation. Dealers are known for their communication skills; these skills can be used in social media as well.

8 *Engage often.* Sharing information is more than just posting information. There is a difference between informing someone and sharing something with them. Sharing is a different level of communication. In many ways, sharing engages your audience on a personal level. Think about a relationship, if all you do is inform your significant other about yourself, what would happen to that relationship? Car dealers are great at talking with people. Use social media to transfer your dealers' real world people skills to the virtual world. Introductions are no longer done with a handshake; often, it happens on a mobile device via text or e-mail. In fact, dealers are saying that more customers come to them from the Internet. "One area we intend to improve on as we head into the next year is communicating with potential customers via text messaging," says Chadd Linnehan of Linnehan's Right Way Auto. "A majority of customers find texting to be more convenient and less intimidating than a phone call. It is really the next evolution beyond email."

9 *Keep it clean.* Make sure your brand is portrayed the way you intend it to be portrayed. In other words, pay attention to what you say and how you say it when you represent your dealership on social media channels; don't post offensive content (videos, images, or text), don't post links to any offensive posts, pay attention to your tone when you write, etc. Remember that you are using social media to communicate with customers and to build positive relationships. As a rule of thumb, don't say or do anything that you wouldn't say or do in person.

SOCIAL MEDIA TASK LIST

Twitter
- Find seven things worth retweeting in your general feed and share.
- Give at least five full responses (not just "thanks").
- Point out a few people that you admire. It shows your mindset, too.
- Follow back at least 10 folks. (You can use an automated tool, but

this is a personal preference. Ex: SocialToo is an automated tool you could use.)

- Ten minutes of just polite two-way chit-chat goes a long way.

Facebook

- Check in on birthdays on the homepage (Send a birthday wish via Twitter or email. It will look even more deliberate).
- Respond to comments on your wall.
- Post a daily status update, something engaging or interesting.
- Comment on at least seven people's statuses or updates.
- Share at least three interesting updates that you find.
- If you belong to groups or fan pages, leave a new comment or two.

LinkedIn

- Accept any invitations that make sense for you to accept.
- Add customers or partners from your business card stash to your Linkedin profile (if you're growing your network).
- Drop into Q&A and see if you can volunteer two to three answers.
- Every few days, recommend at least one person that you can honestly and fully recommend.
- Add any relevant slide decks to the Slideshare app there, or books to the Amazon bookshelf.

Blogs

- Visit your blog's comments section and comment on at least five replies.
- If you have a few extra minutes, click through to the blogs of the commenters, and read a post or two and comment back.
- While on those sites, use a tool like StumbleUpon and promote their good work.
- Write an occasional post promoting the good work of a blog in your community.

Daily Activities

- Monitor social media for keyword hits, respond as needed.
- Monitor alerts for relevant content, post to social media sites as tweets, links and updates.
- Promote company blogs and other content to social networks and bookmark the sites as content is published.

Weekly Activities
- Recruit new followers on the main social networking sites via search and invitations to connect.

Analytics and Reporting
- Evaluate reach (brand awareness), number of new followers and influence (number of posts and retweets by followers).
- Evaluate feedback via comments and other social media engagements.
- Evaluate monitored keywords in conversations and respond to positive and negative comments.
- Adjust topics, quality and quantity of social media engagements to enhance reach, influence and brand reputation.

SEARCH ENGINE OPTIMIZATION

If you have the chance, start researching Search Engine Optimization (SEO). We will cover what SEO is and why it is important in the next chapter. Ask your Web administrator about it. It is important that you start communicating with your website administrator.

Action List

1 Search the Internet and find out the definition of "Facebook Timeline Cover." Create a Facebook Timeline Cover design.

2 Add your timeline cover to your Facebook page. Add your logo to your dealership's Facebook page.

3 Find five Twitter users to follow who aren't celebrities. Tweet something.

4 Claim or create your dealership's Google+ page. Add your logo to your Google+ page.

5 Add or confirm your business address, phone number, email and website address on your Google+ page.

6 Add pictures of happy buyers to your Google+ page.

7 Claim or create your dealership's Yelp page. Call your mom and have her give you a raving review on Yelp. If your mom is busy, have one of your kids do it.

8 Search YouTube for videos about your brands or your competition.

9 Add your logo or a picture to your LinkedIn account.

SUMMARY

Get familiar with the major social media channels. It may all seem new and unfamiliar when you are first creating accounts for your social media channels, but you will get familiar if you don't give up.

Follow the steps and create accounts for channels that you think would benefit your business. Start posting and get accustomed to navigating your new social media outlets. Once you get the hang of it, you will soon be doing tricks. Don't get frustrated when things don't go your way immediately. Remember when you first started doing tricks on your bicycle? It took a few falls before you finally mastered the tricks right? Such is life and the same rules apply to social media, too.

Always remember that you represent your company in all of your channels; being social doesn't mean kicking professionalism out the door!

PUTTING YOUR SOCIAL MEDIA SKILLS INTO PRACTICE

Now that we've discussed the basics in the "Beginner" section, it's time to put what you learned into practice and build up your business using social media! Excited? You should be. This is fun stuff.

Brand Representation

Brand representation is important in social media. We encourage you to use your official logos on all your social media channels. When possible, you should even adjust the colors of your social media platforms to match your official brand. This is easy to do in Twitter.

For Facebook, we suggest that you design several timeline covers for different seasons, events, etc. Changing up your timeline cover will give your "Likes" another reason to check out your page and it will also keep things interesting.

Organization

By now, you should know how to add content to your social media channels. Create a set schedule to help you manage your various social media channels. We recommend creating a calendar that outlines specific tasks. If you use Google Calendar or Outlook, you can add posting dates and times as recurring events and add reminders to keep yourself organized and on track.

There are tools out there that will consolidate content for you; we will discuss more about them in the advanced section. For now, you should be adding at least one blog post every week, a Facebook status update twice a week, and tweeting three times a day.

Accelerating Growth

Most of your energy should be concentrated toward adding followers (who are willing to participate) to your social media channels. We already mentioned adding icons to your website and adding urls to your written media content. This is a good start, but there's more to do!

An easy way to add followers is by bribing them! Everyone likes to get stuff right? There are a lot of ways to do this; we are partial to contests. Contests are a great way to coax followers to your social media channels.

Think about these examples and see if you can draw inspiration!

- During your first month, get your staff to participate in a contest to see who can add the most Likes to your Facebook page. It shouldn't really matter who the Likes are, although, it would be nice if they are prospects and customers. You never know which Like is going to share your content with their 1,000 friends. Make the contest fun!

- In month two, start a contest encouraging prospects and customers to stop by your dealership. Many promotions that worked in the past can work with social media, so test a few to see what happens. If you're going to live in the dealership until you sell 20 cars, let everyone know through social media. Add photos of you sleeping or exercising in the dealership as the promotion continues.

- We have noticed that users respond well to contests that support charities. Maybe you're going to live in the dealership until 400 people stop by the dealership and bring an unwrapped toy for Toys For Tots?

- You can have an annual scavenger egg hunt all over the lot, but add a twist. Put a $100 bill in one egg and promise to triple it if the parent of the kid who finds it is already a Facebook or Twitter follower.

- You can also extend things that you are already doing to your social media channels. Let's use the scavenger egg hunt as an example:

  a A month before the hunt, start announcing about a crazy event that's going to happen on such and such a date at such and such a time and that the only way to get details about it is to like you on Facebook. Put a banner in front of the dealership with your Facebook address and a simple text, like "You Won't Believe What We're Gonna Do Next."

b In your blog and Twitter updates, mention the event without giving any details and add your Facebook page link to your blog post and tweets.

c When you get to the start of the week before the event, start giving out details, but only on your Facebook page. Make sure your Likes are sharing your post with their Likes by saying that, "only our Facebook Likes are eligible for this great event."

d Two days before the event, rent a Bunny suit and put your worst salesperson in the suit for the entire day. You can do this if you had announced a sales contest the previous month, letting your sales staff know that whoever gets the lowest sales will get the costume.

e The day before the event, let all of your Facebook Likes know that you are having a scavenger egg hunt on the lot the next day and that there will be $20, $50 and $100 eggs on the lot. Make it loud and clear that if a Facebook Like finds one of these eggs, you will automatically TRIPLE the value!

f Take lots of pictures and videos on the day of the hunt. Make sure you get pictures of people flashing their cash. Add the pictures to your blog, Facebook page and tweet them on Twitter. Add the video to your YouTube channel and post the link to your Facebook and Twitter pages. Copy the link after you upload the video to YouTube, and when you paste the link in your Facebook feed, the headline from the video and the start screen will automatically appear in your News Feed. It's that easy!

g The next day, add a blog post about how fun it was to host the event and how much you love the community. Then, let them know that something else is coming and that it's even BIGGER!

h This is a simple example of how you can successfully harness social media. The success in this event would be acquiring new followers that you can communicate with via social media. This is only one of the many ways that you can capture an audience, and you may even sell a car of two if your staff is on top of their game.

- Contests and promotions can provide you fresh pictures and videos that will appeal to the community. The fact that Facebook Likes get special treatment will encourage others who hear about the contest to Like your page.

- People usually "Like" a business when they are impressed.

- You can also reverse promote. For example, you can announce on Facebook and your blog that you are giving away tickets to an upcoming concert or sporting event. Announce that the first Twitter follower to correctly identify some obscure car part will get the tickets. Over a period of days, you can send out tweets with hints until you have a winner. As always, make sure you get pictures of the winner and share them on all of your channels.

More Tips and Examples

- If you have a service department, offer your Facebook Likes a free indoor car wash in the middle of winter. They can stroll the showroom while their car gets washed and dried in the warm service bay. You can let the local Girl/Boy Scout troop and the high school band do the washing as a fundraiser. Anyone dropping by your lot will notice all the activity and your staff can explain that only Facebook or Twitter followers get invites to these special services.

- Create a buzz. Let's say you are going to have a "Big Tent" sales event at your dealership. Traditionally, you would rely on newspaper ads to get the word out. However, with social media, you can start the process much earlier. Creating a buzz can help you reach people that you wouldn't normally reach.

- The earlier your audience begins sharing details of your "Big Tent" event, the better. There are companies like Meteor Solutions (MeteorSolutions.com) that can help you create incentives for your event and offer rewards to people who share your event with others.

- Create Twitter #hashtags for your events. As we mentioned earlier in the book, hashtags are simply Twitter names for specific things and are NOT the same as the Twitter owner's name. There is a NFL lineman that has a hashtag just for his beard. His following grew so much that his beard now has its own Facebook and Twitter pages.

- Start by adding your #hashtag to all marketing content you create (i.e. brochures, ads, video, etc.). This will give your audience a way to stay in touch with your event and will help you promote it to other Twitter users. For example, your hashtag could be #BigTent2013 and your tweet could say: "Don't miss the #BigTent2013 event 12/15/2013 10AM-4PM. It's your chance to win a free car from @JoesDealer. Free hotdogs & drinks too. RT" (Check out this tweet's breakdown below).

- Event shaping. It's OK to ask your audience what a perfect car sale should look like. Your audience will be more inclined to participate if you make them feel like they are a part of it or that their opinions matter. So, ask your audience what they want to see and experience via a pool, survey, etc. PollDaddy.com, SurveyMonkey.com, TwtPoll.com are all free services that will help you get input from your customers. Let's face it, buying a new car can be frustrating, scary and intimidating to many folks, so if you listen to your customers and customize the car buying experience to fit their needs, your customers will be more inclined to buy from you and recommend you to their friends and family. So, get a poll going before the event.

Anatomy of a great tweet

Characteristics of a great tweet: informative, readable, contains a marketing hook, has hashtags and contains a call to action. Oh, and it should be no longer than 140 characters–including spaces.

So, let's see how we did with:

"Don't miss the #BigTent2013 event 04/15/2013 10AM-4PM. It's your chance to win a free car from @JoesDealer. Free hotdogs & drinks too. RT"

- Something = Big Tent Event
- Someone = Consumers (general audience)
- Marketing Hook = A chance to win a free car (what is in it for your leads)
- Call to Action = Come see us
- Call to Action = Eat with us (don't worry about lunch that day)
- Call to Action = RT (ReTweet: In Twitter lingo means "Let others know about this")
- Character count = 140
- Hashtag = Yes
- Twitter Address= Yes
- Readable = Yes

So, we did pretty good. If people are interested, they will come. If they are not interested in buying a car, but would like a free meal, they will come for the food. If they are not interested in buying or eating, they may know someone that may be interested, and since you asked them to RT your tweet, they may do that and it will benefit you and your event. So, you ask: How in the world will they know where we are? No worries, they will figure out where to go. When you said @JoesDealer they know that the event is happening there, so when they click on @JoesDealer they will arrive at your Twitter page. If your Twitter page is properly set up, they will see your address, phone number, directions, photos and everything else they need to know as a customer.

TWITTER MANIA
As of this writing there are more than 500 million Twitter accounts!

Social Media Ethics
Effective communication requires trust. So be honest at all times. Don't mislead or misuse the trust your audience puts in you. Be accurate, truthful and transparent in your social media interactions. Remember, just because you type things on a computer doesn't mean that you can say anything you want. The Federal Trade Commission (FTC) is the law of the land with the Internet and hold people accountable when they don't follow.

So, before you post anything on your social media channels, pay close attention to the implications and accuracy of your postings. Statements like, "the best auto dealer in Texas" is broad and may not be accurate and true. On the other hand, a statement like "we guarantee the lowest financing rates in Texas" sounds better, but it better be true, you may find yourself on the FTC's radar.

Disclosure and truthfulness in social media is a must when reaching your audience. Monitor your conversations and immediately correct inaccuracies. Actively implement your social media policy and make sure anyone posting on your behalf understands the gravity of posting inaccurate information. Never pay for reviews and testimonials; keep them real and unforced.

Pay attention to how you respond to the public. It's easy to respond to negative comments with attacks, but it will cost you in the long run.

Your first response to a negative comment should always be something like, "We're sorry you had a bad experience. Please contact us at (your Gmail address) so the owner can personally work with you to make it right."

The Importance of Search Engine Optimization (SEO)

By establishing and improving your search engine presence and ranking, you will increase traffic to your website and eventually to your dealership.

Search Engine Optimization or SEO is one of the best ways to create targeted traffic to your website. With a good SEO plan, your website's pages will attract visitors who are searching for specific keywords and keyword phrases. Targeted traffic gets people who want to see your content to visit your site. As it is in the offline world, when you create a business, you have to tell people about it.

You may not reap the benefits of optimizing your website and social media outlets immediately. It takes time for your website to rank well with SEO. Also, remember that SEO is not a one-time deal; it requires continuous maintenance. There is no single solution to get your website to rank high on Google. Your competitors are most likely doing the same thing you're doing, so if you don't continue to maintain your position, they will snatch it from you. Also, if you don't follow up with your initial SEO plan, it will be a waste of time and money.

We suggest that you get some professional help for your SEO campaign. It is an investment that has the potential of paying off in the long run.

TO-DO LIST

1 Find five citizen journalists. Give a blogger who wants to write about what you are doing the same respect as someone from CNN. The number of bloggers in the world has grown rapidly. Some are good, some, not so much. The World Wide Web and sites like Blogger.com and WordPress have made it easy for anyone to jump into the world of blogging.

    a If you're looking for ways to enhance your content, there are bloggers out there who are willing to post for free. It never hurts to reach out to someone and gauge their interest in contributing articles to your dealership's blog. Be sure to screen their content before allowing the post.

    b A popular site to find writers for your blog is mediabistro.com. From its Freelance Marketplace, you can search by topic (automotive) and see a ton of potential contributors. Most bloggers on the site have examples of their work, so you can get a feel for the blogger's style and decide if they are a good fit for your dealership. Once you build up good content, word of mouth and links can help you reach additional bloggers. It's important to research and read what a blogger writes, including their Twitter, LinkedIn and Facebook accounts. It's like a job interview, but for writing. You need to retain control of the content and your overall blog. So you should closely monitor the content.

2 Segment your audience. Start segmenting your market into three to six distinct categories based on your customers' buying and usage habits. In every business, there are different market segments for different consumers. One person may be looking for a new pickup truck, while another is coming on to the lot to find out about the most fuel-efficient car you offer. Segmenting your market into three to six distinct categories will help you direct your social media content at a higher level of relevancy.

3 Give specific names to your buyer personas. Putting a name and a face (even if they are made up "avatar" types) will help you prepare your content. It can also help you get inside the heads of your audience.

a What are their goals and aspirations? Do they want the most fuel-efficient automobile? Do they need a larger automobile for transporting the family? Maybe they have a large car and want to downsize. Step inside the buyer's shoes and think about their goals and aspirations.

b What are their problems and how can you solve the problems of each group?

c What is their demographic and geographic profile? Where do they live? How old are they? Are they white collar or blue collar?

d What media do they rely on to get answers for their problems? Pay attention to particular media outlets. Are they more likely to read newspaper ads or Google?

e Can you reach them with social media? If they are following your Twitter page, don't be afraid to send a Direct Message via Twitter. Journalists do it all the time to their followers. Example: A recent tweet from the folks at Edmunds.com (@edmunds) said "If you are in the market for a new midsize car, email PR@edmunds.com to talk to a reporter. Thanks!" Something as simple as this can get a great response from your followers. Just make sure the tweet targets your intended audience. You could tweet something like, "We just got a new shipment of Ford F-150 trucks on the lot. Come out and test drive one and receive a free Starbucks gift card." Don't forget to include an image.

BRIDGING GENERATIONS

The fastest growing group of Facebook and Internet users are senior citizens. Once Grandpa figures out that he can keep up with the comings and goings of his grandchildren on Facebook, he's hooked.

4 Know as much as you can about each buyer persona—write their biographies! The more specific you can get with the buyer personas, the better. Answer the following:

5 What words and phrases do buyers use? You know your industry (and your buyers) better than anyone. When they are on your lot, listen to what they are saying. How are they saying it? Ask your staff. What are their main concerns? What are they looking for in a car? Listen closely to what they are saying and take the phrases you hear to create posts for your social media channels.

6 What does each group really buy from you (example: Volvo doesn't just sell a car, it sells safety)? As you know, selling vehicles goes beyond just putting a person in a car. Savvy buyers come to your lot with ideas for their purchase in mind (better gas mileage, more room, less room, more reliable). So, you are not just selling them a piece of metal with four tires. You are selling them a mode of transportation to get to work so they can put food on the table. A reliable ride to drop off and pick up the kids from school. A sense of pride from owning a vehicle. Freedom. Think about the big picture of what you are selling when you sell a car; it goes beyond what you see on a lot.

7 Interview a few customers. Happy customers—especially ones who just bought a vehicle from you. An example can be found on page XX. Note: If you want to use their first name and specific quotes from the interview, have a legal document of consent signed at the end of the interview. Email or call a few customers to request an interview. Once the customer has driven off your lot, it's probably your practice to call and see how everything is going. While you have them on the line, ask if they could answer a few questions about their experience. Be sure to tell them that you intend to use their answers on your social media outlets before they start answering your questions. We're not big fans of comment cards that are mailed to customers. We recommend a more direct and personal approach.

8 You probably already did this, but generate a list of relevant questions for interviews. Come up with a list of approximately 10 interview questions for your happy customers. Include things like: Where do you live? How did you hear about our dealership? What did you like best about your experience? Where is the first place you are going to drive in your new car? You can then take the answers to these questions and post them across the board of social media channels.

9 Add a picture of a new-vehicle owner with their vehicle on Facebook each week.

10 Tweet a great quote from a customer. Don't tweet their full name, just put "I love my new Toyota," says Jessica G.

11 Ask a few service customers what they love about the service department. If your dealership is large, we suggest that you set up separate channels for your service department. The service channels can share content with your regular channels, but they don't have to. Ask a few service customers what they would change, if anything, about their service experience. If you hear a lot of them saying that they wish there was cable TV and a big flat screen, get one. Then promote the "new addition," to the service department and the fact that it was a customer's suggestion.

12 Aggregate all the data you collect into the customer profiles (buyer personas) you created earlier. By now, you should have a clear sense of who your audience is and how to communicate with them.

13 Spend an hour on Wikipedia.com. This is a VERY powerful tool that can improve search engine results of your main website and blog.

14 Write the first Wikipedia article about your dealership, incorporating tips you gathered when you were browsing Wikipedia. For example, Wikipedia articles have a certain structure that starts with a summary, so your article needs to conform to that structure. If a Wikipedia page already exists for your dealership, make sure it is accurate.

15 Spend some time researching Facebook apps. Apps are little pieces of software that attach to Facebook pages and blogs. For example, there are Facebook apps that let you do polling or voting among your Likes. You can use these apps to let your Likes vote on whether they like the old Mustang body style or the new one, etc.

16 Use Google or Bing and research Pay Per Click (PPC) or Adwords advertising. For many dealers, PPC can be a very effective tool for attracting buyers. You may choose to hire a professional to handle your PPC, but you can do it yourself, too.

17 Use Google or Bing and do some research on keywords, keyphrases and long tail keywords. These are ways of determining what potential buyers are typing into search engines and how often they use a particular phrase. (See additional keyoword tips below.)

KEYWORDS AND PHRASES

Your guesses will usually be wrong. Once you have a broad understanding of keywords and phrases, you can use them in your posts and website content. Knowing keywords and knowing how to use them will increase the probability of potential buyers finding your dealership.

Keywords and phrases are also important for your videos and pictures. When you load a video on your YouTube channel, you are given the ability to add a title and description of your video; this is a great place to add a couple keywords or phrases. You will be surprised when one of your videos shows up on the first page of a search.

We don't recommend that you use keywords or phrases that have a bazillion searches every month. The competition for these phrases is intense and sophisticated. You can get better results by focusing on low volume search phrases because they have less competition.

18 Comment on three to five blogs each month, always adding a digital signature to your comment (usually your own blog or website URL). This allows people to find out about you and your company. Some bloggers will even return the favor by commenting on your blog.

19 Monitor what people are saying about your company on blogs, forums and Twitter. Use Technorati and Google Blog Search to search blogs. You can also set up "alerts" in Google and Bing. When you set up alerts, anytime new content pertaining to the specified subject matter is available, you will receive an email from Google or Bing. Alerts are a great way to monitor what your competition is doing and monitor trends within your industry. Avoid broad alerts, such as "car," because your inbox will get filled with useless information. Instead, be specific when you set up an alert. For example: "Volkswagen reviews."

20 Offer gifts to noteworthy bloggers in your industry. Build relationships with those in charge of writing about the industry by offering free copies of your products. A $5 Starbucks card can go a long way.

21 Have a contest and ask customers to produce humorous car sales commercials for your dealership. Offer a good prize, like a GoPro camera. Make sure to note that you reserve the rights to use the submitted videos as you wish, and if you have television spots, use your customer's funny videos creatively.

22 Add your customer's comedic car sales videos to your YouTube channel and promote them on your blog, Facebook and Twitter pages.

23 Review this:

A Dealer who does it right!

We come across many dealers who have embraced the relevance of social media in reaching their customers. Take Tracy Myers of Winston Salem, North Carolina., based Frank Myers Auto Maxx (frankmyersauto.com). He uses his Twitter account @MyersAuto to link his monthly newsletter. He is constantly communicating through Facebook and twitter. His facebook page: www.facebook.com/frankmyersautomaxx has more than 15,000 Likes! It's no surprise that his dealership is successful. His book: Uncle Frank Sez has witty sayings from "Uncle Frank." Not all of us can take social media to Tracy's level (he is a marketing guru), but with a little effort, you can take it to the next level and grow your business.

24 We suggest that you look up the following articles and websites to see how others in the industry are using social media.

25 Find FourSquare.com on the Internet. Register for a personal FourSquare account. Register or claim your business location on FourSquare. Register yourself as "Mayor" of your dealership on FourSquare.

26 Shoot two customer test-drive videos.

27 Load the two test-drive videos to your YouTube channel.

28 Add a post on your Facebook and Twitter accounts with the links to the test-drive video.

29 Learn how to "hide" posts on your blog.

30 Create several QR Codes for your dealership that will direct customers to your main website or social media channels. Have codewords in the pages that are linked to these QR Codes.

31 Announce a QR "scavenger hunt" and use all your social media channels to announce the date and time. Hide small QR Codes all around the dealership; mostly inside cars. The winner must identify all the codewords on the pages linked to the QR Codes. Give out a prize, like a laptop, a smartphone, etc.

32 Go to Pinterest.com and register for an account. After you have confirmed your account, modify it to a business account. Spend 30 minutes surfing Pinterest. Get familiar with Pinterest activities: Likes, Repins, Boards, etc. Follow five Pinterest users; they will probably follow you back.

33 Visit HootSuite.com. Setup and confirm a HootSuite account. We'll be using this account in the advanced section.

34 Find Instagram on your smartphone or on the Internet. Set up and confirm an Instagram account.

35 Link your Instagram account to your Facebook, Twitter and blog accounts.

36 Identify four "safety events," you can host at your dealership. These events are a great way to create foot traffic to the dealership. Foot traffic is important for several reasons— you never know when a conversation will generate a sale and if customers are on your lot, they can't be on someone else's. Finally, you are creating an opportunity to make the prospects feel comfortable with your lot and staff.

Practical Examples
1. *Team up with a local scout troop or school and arrange a free headlight lens cleaning day.* Let customers know they can make a dona-

tion to the partnering organization for your service. Buy toothpaste and scrubbing pads at your local dollar store and get one of your service or detailing people show the scouts how to apply toothpaste to the headlights and gently wipe them clean.

2. *Contact your local fire department and find out if they can recommend someone that does child safety-seat checks.* Set up a day where parents can have their car seats checked for safety. People can give a "boot" donation to the fire department for their service. Have the local police department there as well, so that drivers can ask any traffic or road-safety related questions from the officers.

3. *Have a $1 "bulb check" event.* Anyone who comes in can have any burned out bulb, except headlights, replaced by your service techs. No matter how many bulbs are replaced, the cost is $1. Team up with your parts suppliers and offer headlight replacement for the cost of the headlight.

37 Identify dates to hold your safety events. Announce your safety event schedule to your staff.

38 Use your social media channels to announce each event. Encourage your Facebook Likes and Twitter followers to share the event with others.

39 Research Facebook apps you can use to allow the public to schedule their appointment to each safety event.

40 Announce the ability to pre-register for your safety events via the Facebook app you choose.

41 Take lots of pictures and videos of the safety events.

42 Load the safety event videos to your YouTube channel.

43 Upload the safety event pictures to your Instagram account. Make sure to attach fun captions to each picture.

44 Confirm that the Instagram pictures are loaded to your Facebook and Twitter account.

45 If not, manually add the pictures on Facebook and Twitter with the Instagram link and figure out why the pictures weren't loaded correctly.

46 Spend some time working with Microsoft Movie Maker, Camptasia or other video editing solutions. If your video camera is newer, you may have access to a video editing solution from the camera maker.

47 YouTube.com has a video editing software. Check it out.

48 Talk to your service staff and create a list of the five most frequently asked questions they receive from service customers.

49 Shoot videos of different service techs answering these questions.

50 Create a slide in PowerPoint for each service question. Save each slide as a PNG file.

51 Using Movie Maker, import your title slide and your video. Add the title slide at the beginning and the end of your movie.

IMPROVED VIDEO QUALITY

Using video settings, extend the length of time that the title slide is shown at the end of your movie so that this length is at least 51 percent of the total video length. So, if your video is one minute long, you want the closing title slide to be more than 30 seconds. By doing this, you ensure that you can choose the title slide as the thumbnail view when you load the video to YouTube. You are now improving the quality of your videos and your video channel.

52 Load your finished service-question videos to your YouTube channel and promote the videos on your Facebook, Twitter, Google+ and blog pages. Don't forget to add a few keywords and phrases in your descriptions. Google owns YouTube, so Google loves YouTube.

53 Take some time to meet with the person or company that maintains your main website. Ask them the following:

- Is our website friendly for mobile phone visitors?
- Is our website focused on good lower-volume relevant keywords and phrases?
- Does our main website have good original content?
- If so, does it have enough content?

By now, you may be wondering about the economic value of social media. We will discuss return on investment (ROI) in our next section.

ACTION LIST

In researching this book, we discovered several resources and auto-finance related websites that we thought were great.

Look these up when you get a chance and get some inspiration and ideas:

Best overall use of social media: **Capital One**
Best original blog (tie): **Kicking Tires by Cars.com and Inside Line by Edmunds**
Best use of original online staff-written articles: **TRUECAR**
Best overall Facebook page: **Capital One**
Best use of contributors for original content: AutoTrader
Best overall Twitter page: **American Express**
Best idea for using non-original content: **The Edmunds Daily from edmunds.com**
Best Twitter site used ONLY for customer service: **@AskCapitalOne**
Best use of Twitter to interact with audience: **AutoTrader**
Best use of Facebook to post questions to audience: **AutoTrader**
Best use of questions posed to audience via Twitter: **Ally**
Best use of Google+ to post customer reviews: **RoadLoans.com**
Best use of Facebook for auto dealer contests: **Santander Auto Dealers**

Cars.com
- Blog called Kicking Tires, Tagline The Blog for Car Buyers
- Twitter account -- @carsdotcom
- iPad/iPhone/Android/Mobile App
- Facebook

TrueCar.com and Y! Autos

Look at the blog taglines.

AutoTrader

Autotrader.com is specifically geared toward consumers. AutoTrader's Facebook page has more than 143,000 Likes. They post original articles on industry-related topics. They get customers to communicate by asking questions like "If a sports car gets good fuel-economy, does that make it more or less desirable?" "What is the most important feature you look for when shopping for a family car?" "Why did you purchase your current vehicle?" You should Like the AutoTrader Facebook page. Become a contributor and have your hand on the pulse of the marketplace.

Capital One

Most of their Facebook posts have images. They run polls: What type of shopper are you? Impulse Buyer, Bargain Hunter, Research Junkie, Online Only; and general posts: "The NHL Playoffs are kicking off tonight. Show your team some love if you think they're going to take the Stanley Cup!" Their content is not groundbreaking, but they have a lot of followers.

Capital One is the only financial services brand in socialbakers top 150 Facebook pages chart.

They have disbanded the main Capital One Twitter page and are using a customer service Twitter feed (@AskCapitalOne) that is manned by dedicated reps who spend all day replying to customer tweets (They only have 8,180 Followers). Capital One does not have an official blog.

American Express

Is one of the top financial services brands on Facebook; mostly due to promotions like offering early tickets to sporting events. They have more than 300,000 Twitter followers with many tweets related to Amex-sponsored events and content (film festivals, NBA games, clothing, concert tickets etc.).

Ally

Rather plain in appeerence, www.ally.com does not have many bells and whistles. Their Twitter page, @AllyBank has 16,992 followers. Here are some of their tweets: "Should married couples merge their finances? What would you do?" "What do you think is the best job to have in 2013? Software engineer, financial planner, or HR Manager?" "I was _____ years old, when I opened a savings account." "Identity theft is still the #1 complaint in the US, according to the FTC http://bit.ly/HAsjgu "RT" this if you've never been a victim."

Edmunds
Their Facebook page runs auto news with a unique twist: Top 10 best-selling vehicles, reviews on new cars, etc. Their Twitter page has 51,692 followers. The Edmunds Daily, is put together with content gathered from various sources. They have three blogs:Long-term Road Tests, Readers Rides and Straightline.

MSN Autos
Their blog, Exhaust Notes, covers various industry-related topics and auto reviews. Check out their tagline: "Making sense of your automotive world." Their Twitter page, @MSNAutos has 17,110 followers and "provides the latest automotive news, feature stories, videos and details about thousands of new and used cars." They tweet about four times a day and upload one blog post a day.

SUMMARY

Social media can be very effective if you do it right. We have provided several examples and suggestions that you can use according to your comfort level and needs. Try to implement some of the fine-tuning suggestions provided in this section. The suggestions will help you build a strong social media presence. Learn what you can from the blogs and social media strategies of industry-related organizations that we have discussed. Don't hesitate to do your own research. Be creative when you plan your events. Pay attention to the guidelines we have outlined and work toward building up your audience.

MASTERING SOCIAL MEDIA

In this section, the rubber hits the road and we put social media into high gear. We are going to give you suggestions that will help gauge your social media success. Monitoring social media success will give you a better idea of what you are doing right and what you need to change or improve. The tips and examples provided here are geared toward equipping you with advanced knowledge that will give you a good starting point as you begin to master the art of social media.

In the beginner section, we gave you a task list (pp. 43-48). Now, let's look at that list and start measuring your success! We hope that you added more things to that list. If you do not have a list, take some time and create a list and include what you have been doing as a part of your social media strategy.

Before we dive into measuring your success, there are a few more important things that we would like you to know. These are more advanced operations, functions and management decisions that go beyond social media channels that have strong ties to social media success and effectiveness. So hang tight and don't hesitate to Google if something doesn't make sense. Things like widgets are not that easy to comprehend by just reading. So, it is always a good idea to look for examples to get a better understanding of the subject matter.

Insourcing and Outsourcing
This is a good juncture to discuss insourcing versus outsourcing your social media. Before reviewing your options, let us make a

recommendation: DO NOT ALLOW ANYONE TO TAKE OVER YOUR SOCIAL MEDIA CAMPAIGN WITHOUT YOUR PERSONAL OVERSIGHT. Regardless of the option you choose, you need to keep your hands firm on what is happening. You can loosen your grip over time. But, early on, NOTHING should be added to ANY social media channel without your approval. This is the best way to ensure that you are sending messages that you want to send.

First, let's talk about insourcing. You should consider assigning parts of your social media workload to members of your own staff. Tasks like video editing and loading, tweeting, Facebook posts and event planning can be assigned to the staff.

We suggest that you assign different tasks to different staff members. Why? First, if a staff member quits, you only need to reassign one component of your work. Second, by getting staff to work on independent components that will ultimately connect together, you will create accountability and teamwork.

If you are going to outsource pieces of your social media work, we have a few suggestions. First, do not sign long-term contracts with anyone. The social media landscape changes rapidly and being tethered to a provider that is behind the curve will hurt your campaigns. There are lots of providers that will work month to month.

Second, you should always confirm in writing that all created content belongs to you and you alone. A disgruntled vendor may feel tempted to remove their content when you end the relationship and claim that the content belongs to them. Don't assume it's yours just because it sits in your channel. Without a written agreement, there is no way to claim ownership.

Third, always try to avoid "renting" solutions. You should own your domain. There are many providers who will build a low cost or free website on a domain that belongs to them. Guess what happens when you decide to take your business somewhere else? All your hard work will be lost. It's OK for you to rent hosting space, but own your domains and your sites. If you decide to change hosting providers, it is relatively easy to move your domains and sites to a new provider.

Finally, put it in writing that all providers maintain usernames and passwords that you set up and that any changes will require your written approval. Once every quarter, confirm that you can log into all your social media channels. If you can't log in, have a serious conversation with the provider. Some providers change the username and password when they begin work, then hit you with an exit fee before giving them back.

For website management, event planning and promotion, we suggest that you work with a local partner. Also, confirm that the provider is not working with any of your local competitors; their mixed loyalties will create problems later.

There are many ways that you can outsource content creation and article writing. Do some research and make sure to review work samples before choosing a provider.

Getting the work done has a cost. If you choose to do it yourself, understand that you are probably a very, very expensive solution to the problem. Insourcing may be a little cheaper since you are already paying your staff, but remember that there is a time cost for that too. You may not find the perfect staff members for the tasks, which, in turn, will diminish your success.

Outsourcing cost is easy to measure because your cost is what you pay the agency. Ask around and research some local providers before making a decision.

WEB STRATEGY

What is a Web Strategy?
A Web strategy analyzes and anticipates root causes of online success or failure, and finds solutions. A Web strategy will address the long-term strategic business plan for your online presence.

It is similar to a business plan, but for your website. Here, we will outline a roadmap that will cover obstacles and challenges you might face. How you overcome these obstacles and achieve your goals will determine your success.

Do We Really Need a Web Strategy?
Short answer? Yes. The Web has become extremely important for conducting business. The void between the real world and the virtual world is closing as people's reliance on the Internet continues to grow with each new technological advancement. Your Web strategy can be used to achieve sub-goals that support the ultimate mission of your organization. An effective Web strategy is essential in this media-driven age.

What Questions Does a Web Strategy Answer?
Some examples of Web strategy questions:

What type of customers use your website?
Putting all your customers in one big group is an example of not having a Web strategy. Not all customers are the same.

Does your website satisfy the needs of all types of customers?
Many website owners only think about their own needs. Just like people hate salesmen who only care about commissions, people hate websites that are only focused on sales. Your website should be helpful to customers and make them feel comfortable.

What are the top 10 questions customers ask when they get to your website? How can you answer them?
Websites that fail to answer important customer questions will fall short, because the customers can find a competitor website that will answer important questions.

What action do you expect from the customer on each page of your website?
This will help you make each Web page as effective and purposeful as possible.

How do you determine if getting customers to visit your website is productive?
How are you going to ensure that you get the most out of each visit to your website? Are you trying to get a phone call, a subscription, a purchase, a membership? The answer to this question will greatly affect your entire website layout and design.

What is the average conversion rate for your industry and what is the target conversion rate for your website?
How can you set up a target conversion rate without knowing the average conversion rate for your industry? These numbers are important and you need to find them.

Besides search engine traffic, directories and advertising, what is your six-month plan for increasing the number of visitors to our website?

Millions of websites are competing to get on Google Search, Yahoo Directory, etc. If you do the same thing as everyone else, you will get the same results. The average websites fail. So, what will you do differently?

What are your goals for your website next month? In three months? Six months? One year?
Your goals should guide your everyday activity. "Great ideas" that are not a part of the Web strategy, can impair your capacity to succeed.

What lessons have you learned from your competitors in the last six months?
Your competitors are trying thousands of different things to find success. What can you learn from them? What would you do? What would you never do?

Is there any reason for a customer to tell their friends about your website?
Word-of-mouth is the best kind of marketing that you can get. To get an honest answer, you may need to ask someone else for their opinion. This is one of the most important questions to answer.

Digital Strategy
We encourage you to use a digital strategy to make sure that your dealership is using its online assets effectively. A digital strategy differs from a Web strategy that in that it will help you identify how your dealership can take advantage of the opportunities created by the digital world. Having a clear and concise vision for how you intend to operate in the online world will enable your dealership to be more productive.

Widgets
Now that we have covered the importance of having good Web and digital strategies, we want to point out the importance of widgets. Widgets can drive traffic to your social media channels by creating gateways to your social sites.

A widget is an application that can be embedded in your main website and blog. Widgets come in various forms: clocks, stock market tickers, daily weather, etc. Remember we mentioned that you should work with your web administrator to get your social media icons to your main website? Widgets are a great way to prompt your Web visitors to check out your social media channels. Also, if you have a widget on your blog, visitors can share your blog content on their social media channels. Creating opportunities for visitors to create your content on their social media channels will drive more traffic.

It is easier to place widgets on a blog (depending on the blog platform) than it is to embed them to a web site. So, you may need to contact your web administrator to get it done. It is worth it!

Questions to Answer

We suggest that you answer these questions and find a strategy that works best for your dealership.

1 What opportunities are you not using? What are your competitors doing? Ask these questions from those that directly and indirectly influence your dealership. This includes senior management, customers, dealers, etc.

2 Are all of your customers satisfied? What can you do to meet your customers' needs? There are so many ways to get customer feedback. We encourage you to dig deep when answering this question. As we mentioned earlier, customers drive the marketplace, so it is extremely important that you know what the customers think.

3 What is your vision for the online component of your business? The Internet is a key player today. How does your real life vision translate to the virtual world? Are they compatible? You may have to create a separate vision for the Internet if it isn't. Of course, the two visions should be in harmony, but since how your business operates in the two realms is different, they may not look exactly the same.

Once you have found answers to these questions, figure out how you are going to change what needs to change and implement your strategy effectively.

Role of Personas in Digital Strategy

You can use the personas that you created to get general ideas about what your customers may be looking for. Various research methods such as surveys and interviews can be used to gather data to create personas. These personas can serve as reference points when you create your digital strategy. Knowing your audience is important in the digital world. Building personas is a great way to overcome the barrier of not being able to physically see your customers in the virtual world. Paying attention to customer behavior can help you identify customer needs and your digital strategy should attempt to meet those needs as much as possible.

Executing Your Digital Strategy

Test your website extensively using various methods. Make sure to test the effectiveness of your changes before you publish them. Remember, you're catering to your customer's needs, so try to get a few people that fit your personas to tryout your website. Take good notes and figure out how you can make your website more user friendly. Pay close attention to details. Make sure that your average customer does not get confused or overwhelmed when they go to your website.

A SUMMARY OF SOCIAL MEDIA GUIDELINES

- Social media is not so much about marketing; it is more about communication and networking.

- Be authentic. Be casual but don't lose your professionalism. Learn from others. As we mentioned earlier, you can learn a lot from your competitors' successes and failures. Don't forget that real life courtesy and respect applies to social media too. In fact, you need to make more effort to portray your dealership in a positive light when you communicate via social media, because on social media, people go by what they see and read, not by what they hear and feel. So, make positive relationships and build a strong network of followers.

- Don't be self-centered. Don't use your social media channels to constantly promote your dealership. Remember, every time you post something, your dealership is either directly or indirectly promoted. So, don't overdo it. Same rules that apply for relationship building in real life should apply to social media too. After all, social media is used by real people, so it is important to keep in mind to pay attention to how you conduct yourself on your social media channels. We are not too fond of boasting or narcissistic self-promotion in real life right? So, why would you want to be that way on social media?

- Be social. Don't be a boring company that always tries to get people to come out and buy something. Share with your followers and try to humanize your dealership. A personal touch can make your followers feel like they are being heard and make it easier for them to communicate with you. Your dealership is not just another business, it is made up of interesting people. So think of ways you can show the human aspect of your dealership.

- If you see an opportunity to share something helpful with your audience, don't hesitate to do so. Communicate without hidden agendas. People appreciate openness. Always remember that what you say and how you say it will affect how your audience perceives your dealership.

-

BE S.M.A.R.T.[2]

Specific	Special
Marketable	Measurable
Attainable	Accurate
Relevant	Relationship Driven
Timely	Tasteful

Specific & Special
- What do I want to achieve? Is this unique? Why would anyone read this? Review and understand the specificity and uniqueness of your campaign's environment. RESEARCH before engaging.
- Just like you won't jump into dark waters without basic precautions and headlamps, don't begin your social media networking campaign without proper planning and precautions. Diving recklessly into social media can turn out to be a total mess, especially when it comes to building awareness and product reputation. Building an effective online social strategy requires thorough knowledge of how competitors operate as well. So, research and observe successful and failed social media strategies. You can learn a lot from other people's mistakes.

GET TECHNICAL
Learn more about the technical potential of each media platform.

Marketable & Measurable

- Is your commentary going to help you market something? Can you measure the outcome? What do you want your audience to do? Review and understand how your engagement can be justified.
- Time is money. Running a dealership these days requires social media involvement. It's all about making a profit, and for that to happen, your engagement needs to be fun, spontaneous and focused. To make it measurable, you must include a call-to-action in your engagement. Are the results of your goal measurable? Finding analytical data to measure the success of a goal isn't always easy.

Attainable & Accurate

- Is the goal of this post attainable and realistic? Is this post accurate? Review and understand the business impact of what you are about to do.
- Only realistic goals can be measured. No matter how awesome an idea is, it will be effective only if it is implemented correctly. As with all great things in life, execution is crucial. Make sure your goal is always realistic. If you are posting a statement, make sure your post is accurate and truthful.

Relevant & Relationship Driven

- Is my post relevant, new and exciting? Would I want to read this? Once I read, would I feel compelled to pass it along to family and friends?
- Let's face it. The Web offers a lot of junk. Providing good and relevant content will naturally grab people's attention. Once you have their attention, the goal is to build a strong professional relationship. You want your followers and fans to participate, repost and engage as advocates of your business.

Timely & Tasteful

- Am I overthinking this? Is this post disclosing any sensitive information?
- Many companies suffer from a condition called Analysis Paralysis. So, make your engagement tasteful and know your audience. Be careful about what you post. Remember that you are representing a dealership and assess the tone, voice and message of your posts.

Social Media Guidelines
Be S.M.A.R.T.2 CHEAT SHEET

1   Am I signed in to the correct account?

2   What do I want to achieve?

3   Is this unique enough? Would anyone want to read it?

4   Is my commentary going to help us market something?

5   What do I want my audience to do?

6   Is the goal of this post attainable and realistic?

7   Is this post accurate, relevant, new and exciting?

8   Would I want to read this and pass it along to family and friends?

9   Am I overthinking this?

10 Is this post in compliance with the dealership's social media policy?

MEASURING SOCIAL MEDIA SUCCESS

As we stated earlier, social media strategies must be measurable. Since hard data comes in many forms, there are many ways to measure your success. Here are a few examples:

- Added Facebook Likes, Twitter followers and website page views.
- Improved search engine rankings. Did your website move up, down or is it at a standstill?
- Actual audience attendance at your events.
- Number of guest postings on your blog.

Use a checklist: did you do everything that you scheduled for your social media channels this month?

All of these examples allow you to measure success using real data.

You either hit the mark or you don't. The fact that you didn't hit a particular mark does not necessarily mean that you failed. It might mean that your goal was too aggressive and that it needs to be adjusted. If this is the case, adjust the goal for the next month and measure it again.

Since you run a dealership, the ultimate measure is vehicles sold and service/parts revenue.

We suggest a funnel approach when measuring social media success. For example, new Facebook Likes will be at the broad end, and the number of car sales will be at the narrow end and your events, contests, promotions, etc. will be in between. Before you decide that your social media campaign is or isn't working, we want to remind you that there are factors that you can and can't control that will contribute to success or failure.

Let's use the U.S. economy as an example. When the economy started to tank, new-car sales plummeted and used-car sales roared. But, because some people were holding onto their vehicles, the available number of used cars started to drop, causing the cost to rise. After a while, new-car sales rebounded. You can't control these changes, but you can use these changes to your advantage. If the changes affect buyers, why not write a blog post on how customers may be affected and suggest a few things that they could do about it? It's highly unlikely that you will cause a buyer to delay a new or used vehicle purchase because many of these buyers are being pressed by other factors; like a huge impending service bill, to make a change. So, you may give delaying buyers a reason to buy sooner.

If you read the *tea leaves* and saw that used-car prices were going to rise (and it wasn't hard to see that coming), you could encourage folks who are looking to buy a used car to NOT wait much longer. Then, you could offer them an incentive, like free gas, to bring them in.

There are also factors that you can control that you may be already controlling. If you have segmented your buyers, you can adjust your inventory to reflect their specific needs. If many of your buyers are young married couples, "safe and fuel efficient" will get their attention. So, make sure that your social media channels convey this message.

Assigning a strict return on investment (ROI) to your social media campaign is difficult. But, there are a few things that you can add to the equation to help.

GET A SPECIFIC MEASUREMENT

Measuring the number of overall Facebook Likes is a general measurement, while measuring how many Facebook Likes you acquired because of an event is more specific.

Your primary goal is to listen and engage with the social media universe and interact with customers that are interested in your products. Your secondary goal is to increase traffic to your dealership. Look at the template we have provided below to get some ideas of how you can improve your social media strategy and measure success. Feel free to add to it. Use this template as a guideline. We encourage you to create your own!

SOCIAL MEDIA STRATEGY MEASUREMENT TEMPLATE

General
- Decide on the overall vibe you want to create
  - A personal approach ("I" instead of "We")
- What does your dealership do best?
  - Cars, trucks, etc.
- Find two employees to work full time on social media

Blog
Objectives
- Increase recognition:
  - Create a blog publication schedule
  - Add RSS button to your news articles, effectively creating FFA syndicated content
  - Post a blog once a day; if not at least once a week
  - Follow up on previous posts once a day
- Increase engagement:
  - Encourage comments, forum pages, FAQs, etc.

Ways to measure success:
- Number of posts
- Audience growth—unique and returns
- Conversation rate

- Conversions
- Subscribers
- Inbound links
- Technorati, Alltop, and other directory listings
- SEO Improvements

Social Networks
Objectives
Create, maintain and expand pages that will engage users and expose them to your dealership.
- Facebook fan page:
  - Create a group, encourage interaction, create content, make sure everyone at the dealership with a Facebook account Likes your page
  - Participate in other groups
  - Explore Facebook Ads
  - LinkedIn
  - Create a group, encourage interaction, create content
  - Participate in Q&A, other groups, etc.

Ways to measure success
- Referrals from social networks
- Friends on social networks
- Followers

Microblogging (Twitter)
Objectives
- Compile a list of Twitter users
- Promote your blog posts on Twitter
- Build reputation
- Promote other social networking activities/sites through Twitter

Ways to measure success
- Friends/Followers
- Second-order followers (follower's follower count)
- Follower engagement—average. number of retweets
- Influence of Twitter followers
- Klout Score—how much influence (reach) is invested in the number of followers
- Pages ranking on key terms from Twitter site

Social Press (Blogger, WordPress)
Objectives
- Update bloggers on a regular basis about news and new products/ services available
- Interact with (plus interview, video, etc.) relevant marketing conferences and local events

Ways to measure success
- Posts by social press related to your dealership
- Referrals from social press

Widgets
Objectives
- Creation of widgets (social media channels, monthly payment calculator, event calendar)
- Distribution of widgets

Ways to measure success
- Usage of widgets (by count)
- Posts/Mentions about social widgets off-site
- Referrals from off-site widgets (if any)

Bookmarking/Tagging
Objectives
- Engage with the following services:
  - Delicious
  - Google bookmarks
  - Reddit
  - Digg
  - Stumbleupon
  - FriendFeed
- Review blog sources to identify additional bookmarking sites that may drive traffic

Ways to measure success
- Referrals from bookmarking/tagging sites
- Pages ranking on key terms from bookmarking/tagging sites

Commenting/Forums/Wikis/Rating and Review sites

Objectives

- Participate in known Marketing wikis. Providing information about your dealership
- Identify additional high traffic discussion boards/forums/wikis
- Comment on posts related to lead management, lead nurturing, email marketing and lead scoring

Ways to measure success

- Referrals from discussion boards/forums/wikis/rating and review sites
- Pages ranking on key terms from discussion boards/forums/wikis/ rating and review sites

Online Video

Objectives

- Update videos on social video sites and link to core site:
  - YouTube
  - Facebook
- Create video series for YouTube

Ways to measure success

Referrals from social video sites

Views of videos on social sites

Pages ranking on key terms from YouTube

Photo sharing

Objectives

- Encourage employees to share any interesting and marketing relevant photos from social marketing or sales events
- Take pictures of any relevant marketing events
- Utilize photo sharing sites to share images with links back to blog and core site:
  - Flickr
  - Facebook Photo Gallery
  - Picasa
  - Google+

Ways to measure success

- Number of likes, shares and comments
- Number of views

Measuring Success

Here are some ways that you can measure the overall success of your social media campaign. Look through this list and create your own template for measuring your social media success. You know what is most important to your dealership and how much effort was put into implementing your strategy. So, it is important that you create your own measurement template.

1 Sales (measured by the total increase in sales indicates the best ROI)

2 Fans (measured by the total number of Likes on Facebook)

3 Followers (measured by the total number of connections)

4 Friends (measured by the total number of friends who circled you on Google+)

5 Subscribers (measured by the total number of subscribers to your page, blog or channel)

6 Recommendations (measured by the total number of people who +1 your posts on Google+)

7 Re-recommendations (measured by the total number of shares of your posts)

8 Consumer created posts (Measured by the total number of consumer-created posts)

9 Competitive shared posts (measured by the number of posts compiled from your posts)

10 Comparative shares (measured by the total number of shares in comparison to other shares)

11 Traditional media mentions (measured by the total number of traditional media mentions (e.g. TV))

12 New media mentions (measured by the total number of new media mentions (e.g. blogs))

13 Uploads (measured by the total number of uploaded content (i.e. contest photos))

14 Downloads (measured by the total number of downloaded content (e.g. white papers, images, etc.))

15 Growth rate (measured by the growth rate of fans, followers, friends, subscribers, etc.)

16 Page views (measured by the total number of unique pageviews)

17 Visitors (measured by the total number of unique visitors)

18 Bounce rate (measured by the total number of people who visited you and left your site immediately after that particular page)

19 Users by Frequency (measured by the total number of unique users by frequency (i.e. How many times the content was viewed by a particular user))

20 Bookmarks (measured by the total number of bookmarks on Delicious.com, Google bookmarks, etc.)

21 Comments (measured by the total number of comments on your blog post)

22 Ratings (measured by total number of "stars" on your YouTube video)

23 Embeds (measured by the total number of times your video was embedded on other sites)

24 Virality (measured by the total number of times your video went viral)

25 Reach (measured by the total number of people reached by your post, tweet or video)

26 Search Engine Rankings (measured by the impact of social media)

27 Linking activity (measured by the total number of social media links appearing on search engine)

28 Klout True Reach (measured by how many people you influence)

29 Klout Amplification (measured by how much you influence other people)

30 Klout Network Impact (measured by the influence of your network)

31 Multimedia shares (measured by the total number of videos, audio and images shared)

32 Influence shares (measured by the total number of shares by influencers (i.e. shares by bloggers))

33 Geographic participation (measured by the total number of geolocations engaged)

34 Segmented participation (measured by the total number of segmented audience engaged)

35 Profile participation (measured by total number of profiles engaged)

36 Persona engagement (measured by the total number of personas engaged)

37 Brand involvement (measured by the total number of brands engaged in social channels)

38 Brand association (measured by the total number of brands associated in social channels)

39 Engagement (measured by the total number of people talking about your posts, tweets and streams)

40 User answers (measured by the total number of user generated answers to other users questions)

41 Female participation (measured by the percentage of females who actually saw posted content)

42 Male participation (measured by the percentage of males who actually saw posted content)

43 Age group participation (measured by the percentage of each age group who saw posted content)

44 Countries (measured by the total number of people broken down by countries)

45 Cities (measured by total number of people broken down by cities)

46 Languages (measured by the total number of people broken down by languages)

47 Tab views (measured by the total number of times each of your tabs were viewed)

48 External referrers (measured by the total number of times people arrived at your page from an external URL)

49 Paid Reach (measured by the total number of people reaching you from paid ads)

50 Organic Reach (measured by the total number of people reaching you from organic sources)

51 Targeted audience engagement (measured by the demographics of specific audience targeted)

52 Follower to Following Ratio (measured by the number of Followers divided by the number of Following)

53 Tweets to ReTweets Radio (measured by the total number of Tweets sent divided by the number of ReTweeted content

54 Twitter top uses

55 Twitter top URLs (measured by the total number of shared URLs)

56 Twitter mentions (measured by the total number of mentions (i.e. @YourName) you got)

57 Twitter replies (measured by the total number of replies sent to your account)

58 Twitter trends (measured by the total number of trends somewhat related to your business)

59 Twitter Direct Messages (measured by the total number of DM sent to you)

TWITTER ANALYTICS / VIDEO REVIEWS

BEST TWITTER ANALYTIC TOOLS
http://twittertoolsbook.com/10-awesome-twitter-analytics-visu-alization-tools/
[Add QR Code of the above link here]
Top 10 Twitter Interface Tools
1. Web
2. HootSuite
3. TweetDeck
4. Gremln
5. Radian6
6. Seesmic
7. Echofon
8. Posterous
9. Disqus
10. Klout

VIDEO REVIEWS
The idea is to get customer reviews on video.
Here is a sample email you can send to your customers:
Using your camera phone, record a review video about your experience at our dealership. Your testimonial should be 20 seconds to a minute long. Once your video is ready, email your video and the authorization form (below) to youremailaddress@yourdealership-name.com. We may post it on our YouTube channel for all to see.

For your time and effort, we will email you back a $25 gift card.

The gift cards will be sent to the email from which received the video review and authorization form. So, make sure to add our email address to your "safe list."

Don't worry about making a perfect video review. We are not looking for perfect. A smile and a few words are enough for us.

Your video review could be about:
• Your new car
• What you will do with your new car
• If you got declined by other auto dealers
• How our auto dealer made buying a car easy
• Your overall experience at our dealer

Examples of what other companies are doing:

THE GRAND FINALE — ACTION LIST

1 Itemize a list of everything related to social media, including steps to complete each task.

2 Assign measures to each task.

3 Monitor your success and make adjustments if necessary.

4 Interview staff and vendors before making outsource or insource decisions.

5 Revisit your HootSuite account and link your blog, Facebook and Twitter feeds together.

6 Test the scheduling feature in HootSuite and confirm that you can use it correctly. Once you master the scheduler, you can load a month's worth of content and you will be done for the month ahead.

7 As you move forward, start forecasting your content early until you can load three months' worth of content at a time.

8 Research press releases and websites that will accept and post them. Study format and structures for press releases.

9 Develop a list of local media contacts.

10 Write your first press release.

11 Submit your press release to your local media contacts.

12 Submit your press release to press release submission sites.

13 Add a Google Alert for any variation of your dealership's name and your name.

14 Check Yelp at least once a month. Because you have been encouraging customers to give you great reviews, you should see your overall score rising.

15 Check your Google+ ratings.

16 Respond to any negative reviews on Yelp and Google+ as soon as you see them.

17 Confirm that your main website has buttons that will lead visitors to your social media channels: Facebook, Twitter, Foursquare, Pinterest, Google+ and YouTube.

18 Research autoresponders, such as MailChimp and Constant Contact. Autoresponders are applications that you can use to automate email marketing, customer satisfaction measurement and loyalty programs.

19 Consider ways that you can use an autoresponder to help your social media campaigns. For example, if someone signs up on your website to receive your newsletter, the autoresponder will record their email address, send them a thank you for signing up and add them to the list of newsletter recipients. You will be renting an autoresponder service, but autoresponder costs are very, very low.

20 Sign up for an autoresponder service of your choice.

21 Build a test email campaign that sends out two emails, a few days apart, after a customer signs up for a newsletter.

22 Confirm that the test was successful. If not, use the customer service number for the provider and let them guide you through and identify where the test went wrong. Major autoresponders provide excellent customer service.

23 Add one vehicle listing to your social media channels each week.

Read the following publications to keep up with auto industry news and get ideas for future social media content:
- Usedcarnews.com
- Autoblog.com
- Autonews.com
- AutoDealerMonthly.com
- AutoRemarketing.com
- DealerTradeNews.com
- AutoFinanceNews.net
- Non-Prime Times

SUMMARY

We covered a lot of important material in this section. When expanding your social media network and reach, you can either insource or outsource content production. We hope that the suggestions and the examples provided in this book will help you make an informed decision. Do some research and see what needs to be done at your dealership, so that you can stand apart from your competition. Look at the templates provided in this section, they will help you strategize and analyze your social media networks effectively. You don't have to adhere strictly to the templates, the idea is to get you to dig deep into the world of social media and to sell more vehicles in the process.

RECAP

We have tried our best to address key elements of social and media marketing for auto dealers. In the social media universe, new tools will emerge and existing tools will fade away. So, we chose to focus on channels that have stood the test of time and are more likely to survive the years to come.

Our suggestions are accurate as of the date of this writing. Some channels like Facebook and Google+, change things up now and then. These changes may affect you, but you'll rarely know until they occur. If you are affected, simply adjust your strategy and keep moving forward.

You can employ as much or as little of our suggestions as you like. One thing we can say with a very high level of certainty is that you simply can NOT ignore social media. If you ignore social media, customers may forget you and prospects will ignore you.

We encourage you to share your social media success stories with us. Also, feel free to send us any questions. Our goal is to help you master the social media landscape!

LOOKING TO
THE FUTURE

As generations move on, the new wave of people that marketers must target are the "millennials," also known as Generation Y. The way that this group of 18- to 34-year-olds perceive advertisements is completely different than their parents and grandparents.

This is where the future of social media continues to unfold, and there are new ways that companies, specifically auto dealerships, can market their products and services to this new age group.

Social media has come a long way in the past 10 years. First came Facebook and Myspace as the new outlets to interact with people over the Internet. Then the Twitter wave came along and revolutionized the efficiency at which people can try to get a point across to their followers. Today, the new ways of interacting with people across social media, in addition to the traditional Facebook and Twitter, are the visual aids that come from social media outlets: Instagram and Vine.

These two relatively new applications combine the use of pictures and videos to get their point across, with the efficiency of Twitter. Because of the visual aid that Instagram and Vine provide, along with the ease of use of the two, they have now become the future of social media marketing and have established themselves as the latest tools of choice for "Generation Y."

Mobile technology has, and will continue to revolutionize how millennials consume media and information. Today's smartphones can perform the same tasks that a computer 10 years ago could, with ease. This means that your auto dealer website needs to be optimized for smartphones. Truth is, some folks might never access your website through a computer! They might not access your website at all! That is why having a social media presence is crucial for success. In short, reaching millennials will require you to cater to their needs, speak their language and even change your strategies!

The millennials

There are 72 million Americans between the ages of 18 and 34. Their buying habits are different from their parents and grandparents. Sixty-three percent of these millennials use social networks to keep updated with brands.

By 2025, millennials will make up 75 percent of the global workplace, and that's why it's extremely important to know how to reach them. The traditional push marketing is proving to be unsuccessful in creating brand awareness and recognition in the tech-savvy — always connected — individual. Hey, think about it, these folks have access to look for what they need, anytime, anywhere! If they are interested in a car, before they even think about walking into a dealership, they will announce it on one, or all, of their social media channels. We've seen it happen over and over again.

Social media has empowered and enabled consumers to spread the word about brands. A brand's ability to control and shape a message has been drastically reduced, given that individuals can do their own research and even conduct opinion polls of what brand is best using their social network.

Millennials and car buying

Studies show that millennials are less eager to get behind the wheel. A National Household Travel Survey conducted by the Federal Highway Administration shows that 16- to 34- year-olds drove 23 percent fewer miles per capita in 2009, when compared to 2001.

According to CNW research, that tracks the auto industry, in 2011 only 27 percent of new cars were bought by 21- to 34-year-olds, down from 38 percent in 1985.

Don't look at these figures and get disheartened. Much of the cause for this reduction in car buying is attributed to lack of funds and car-sharing services like Zipcar. In order to entice millennials to buy cars, manufacturers like Dodge and Hyundai have offered crowdfunding programs, which have shown some success with millennials. Crowdfunding is an online fundraising platform where donations can be solicited by friends and family to finance a car purchase.

One thing is clear: Millennials are very different from their parents and grandparents when it comes to buying and driving cars. But, they are the future. Therefore, they cannot be ignored.

So how can an auto dealer use social media channels such as Instagram and Vine to capture the attention of the millennials?

Research done by Jay Baer, author of *YOUtility*, shows that a consumer gathers 18 pieces of online information before visiting a dealership to buy a car. So your goal should be to show up positively in as many of those impressions.

> **Crowfunding** is an online fundraising platform where donations can be solicited by friends and family to finance a car purchase.

Before we get into how you can use Instagram and Vine to reach millennials, check out these insights from AutoTrader:

- For millennials, it is important that their car represent their personality and accomplishments.
- Younger millennials derive vehicle satisfaction from style and features while the older millennials go for safety and performance.
- 72 percent of younger millennials consider infotainment features as "must-haves."
- Millennials are most likely to be introduced to the car they purchase through family and friends. They depend on word of mouth more than previous generations.
- They also enjoy browsing the dealer lot more than other generations and are more likely to use a mobile device in their shopping process.
- Millennials rely more on salespersons for information, but are likely to go out of their way to avoid interacting with a salesperson.

INSTAGRAM

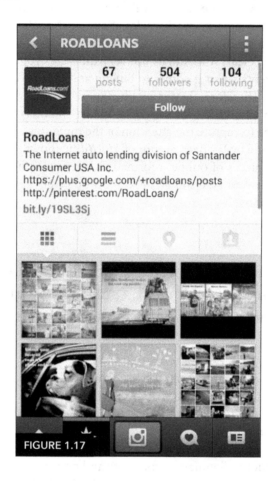

FIGURE 1.17

Kevin Systorm and Mike Krieger drew their inspiration from the Polaroid camera when they created Instagram. Today, Instagram has around 10 million total users that upload an average of 14 photos per second.

Instagram (Fig 1.17) is a free mobile app that can be easily downloaded to your smartphone. Once you create an account, you can share photos and videos. Think of Instagram as a way to tell a story using photos and short video clips.

Hashtags are very important in Instagram. Hashtags are what gets your post to audiences and create interaction. In Instagram, visually pleasing images such as sunsets, nature and "selfies" get a lot of likes.

Birchbox (Fig 1.18) is an example of a company that uses Instagram creatively and successfully. They have over 60,000 followers. Take a look at their Instagram page and make notes of the type of images that they post. Also, click on a few images and read through the comments and see what the followers are saying about the images.

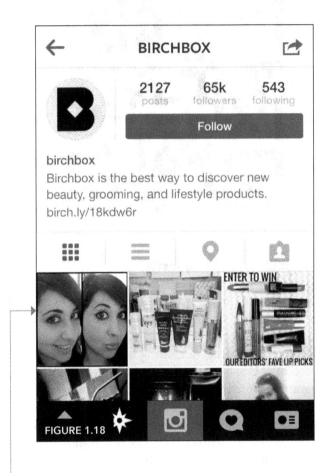

FIGURE 1.18

WHAT'S A "SELFIE"?

A selfie is a self-portrait photograph, usually taken using a hand-held digital device.

Access the QR Code below and browse through all Instagram photos tagged with #dealership. This is a good way to get introduced to what others in your industry are doing with Instagram.

How to reach millennials using Instagram

Just as change is inevitable, sooner or later, reaching millennials will have to be done according to how they (millennials) prefer to be reached. If you are serious about tapping into this market, you simply cannot afford to ignore the social media trends and habits of millennials.

Millennials love Instagram. According to a Pew Internet Research survey, 20 percent of U.S. Internet users aged 18 to 29 were posting photos on Instagram in December 2012. Now add the 14 percent of the 30- to 49-year-olds that did the same! That's a whopping 34 percent!

For an auto dealer that is surrounded by hundreds of shiny, new, souped-up cars, creating a following on Instagram should be a piece of cake. Pictures of automobiles are visually pleasing, and being visually pleasing is very important on Instagram.

We have compiled a few things to keep in mind when broadening your Instagram presence:

Upload genuine content, consistently: Make sure the content does not appear as spam. Building credibility is important. Make it fun. There are so many pictures posted every second, it is important that your content is fun and engaging. It needs to appeal to the younger generation. So, instead of taking straight-on pictures, look for interesting angles when you snap a photo. Here are some tips:

- A close-up of the wheels/rims
- The dashboard
- Headlights
- Don't forget to add a filter and play around with the other features available on the app. Make it look cool!

Post interesting images of your dealership staff: Lifestyle photos with visual appeal do well on Instagram. Ask your staff for interesting ideas. You can even post a short video clip. Always remember to be funny and entertaining. Don't forget that millennials are not big fans of hard sale marketing. So remember to not be too pushy or "salesy" when you post on Instagram.

Do the folks at the dealership have pets? Take photos of their dogs, cats and exquisite animals next to your showroom car. Show how unique you and your staff are.

Use hashtags: Using hashtags will enable you to reach a wider range of audiences. Say you are posting a picture of a new vehicle that just arrived. For the hashtag, you can use something like: #Newarrival #DodgeCharger #sweetride.

Create your own hashtag for your dealership: This way, you can tell folks that visit your dealership to use this hashtag when they post pictures to their Instagram account. At first, if you are trying to grow your account, you can even give a small incentive to folks who use this hashtag.

Link other social media accounts: You can connect your Instagram account to your Facebook page and find more followers. This will give your account a boost to start off. Include your website and other social media channels when applicable. For example, you can have a link to your Facebook page in the description of your Instagram page. Also, you can use the image captions. But be careful, millennials do not like to feel as if they are interacting with a marketer. Everything done on Instagram has to be done with a "soft sale" mentality.

Practical example

Contests are a great way to create brand awareness without being too "salesy" on Instagram, and running an Instagram contest is easy.

The next time you have a special event at your dealership, announce that at the end of the day the dealership will pick the best event photo tagged with your dealership's hashtag. This will help your Instagram page get some followers, and most importantly, potential customers!

This is just one example of what you can do to reach millennials on Instagram. You know your customers best. So cater to their interests.

Also, check out tools that are specifically designed for running contests on Instagram.

HELPFUL TOOL FOR CONTESTS

Wishpond.com is one of many platforms out there that are great for running photo and video contests

Instagram round up

Instagram is a creative space. Instagram users make connections with images and short videos. Keep in mind to be creative and add to this creative hub, where good content will get noticed, fast! Have a soft sale marketing approach when it comes to Instagram. Add value to the community and you will do just fine.

As it is with all other social media channels, there are spammers who overload this space with all sorts of information. Set yourself apart from spam by posting genuine content. Identify a few creative individuals at your dealership and see if they are interested in heading up your Instagram page.

VINE

Vine (Fig. 19) was released to the social media world on January 24, 2013, and is an app that allows you to create and post short videos that cannot exceed six seconds in length. This forces an efficient mode of marketing, which is one that "millennials" like, short and to the point. You can "Like" Vines and you can also re-Vine, which shows other peo-

FIGURE 1.19

ple's Vines on your account.

The idea of Vine was created in June 2012, bought by Twitter in October 2012, and finally released in January 2013. The great thing about Vine is that you can post them to your Twitter and Facebook accounts, making them accessible to your followers.

As of August 2013, Vine has approximately 40 million users, many of whom would be grouped into the category of being a millennial. While most people who have Vine use it for personal videos, the growth for Vine has huge potential as companies are starting to use Vine as a source of advertising and marketing.

How to reach millennials using Vine

Vine, like all other social media applications, is used heavily by those who are between the ages of 18-34 and it can be easily downloaded to any smart phone. Millennials crave the creativity and the excitement that is associated with creating a Vine. Because of this, it is very important that when you are creating a Vine for marketing purposes that you are as creative as possible. A Vine that lacks creativity and excitement will not draw much attention, thus your marketing effort will suffer.

Another important feature to think about when using Vine for marketing purposes, which is similar to Instagram and Twitter, is to create a hashtag for your company, campaign or event, so that you can be distinguished from everyone else. This will also make marketing your product easier because viewers will know exactly what and who they are watching.

Millennials love the new age, high-tech form of marketing and advertising and that is exactly what Vine brings to the table. Important things to think about when making your Vine are creativity, linking to your other social media outlets, and hashtagging which will all help you increase your audience on Vine.

Creativity

- The important thing about Vine is that you have to be creative. Because you only have six seconds to get your point across, you want to create something that will make a lasting impression instantly and make viewers want to watch the Vine two, three, or even four more times, which will leave them craving for more.
- Utilize all your resources in your Vines. This includes employees, cars, and sales that you might have going on.
- Think outside the box. Millennials crave excitement and entertainment, not just another boring commercial.
- Be creative and consistent with Vine, but do not be too overbearing. No one likes to have their Vine feed clogged with the same person or company over and over again. Pick two or three times maximum during the day, and make your Vines count.

Other Social Media Outlets

- One of the major benefits of Vine is its ability to link up to Facebook and Twitter accounts, which typically have more followers and have been around longer.
- Use this to your benefit. Every Vine that is made should be linked with your Facebook page and Twitter account, which will boost views even more, thus giving you more followers and more likes.
- If your Vine account is brand new, posting videos to Facebook and Twitter are great places to start.

Hashtagging

- Like Twitter and Instagram, hashtagging is a vital part of using social media in the most efficient way possible.
- Create your own hashtag for Vine so that viewers will have a solid understanding for what you're going for and it allows for viewers to see all of your videos.
- Using hashtags consistently will help gather a larger audience for your Vine account.

On September 9, 2013, Dunkin' Donuts became the first company to use Vine as a single television advertisement when they launched the ad during the first Monday Night Football of the 2013 season between the Philadelphia Eagles and the Washington Redskins.

Practical Example

Like with all other social media outlets, contests are a great way to engage your audience while promoting your brand.

An easy example for a car dealership to do is promote a sale that your dealership is having at the present time. Let your customers know that whoever creates the most creative Vine with the most likes will receive a discount on a car from the dealership. However, in order for them to participate they must follow your Vine and the Vine must have a specific hashtag of your designation.

This is one of many ways that you can use Vine to promote your business and dealership while engaging your audience in a fun way. Your audience will be pleased that you are paying attention to the customer and this will build your reputation as a company and as a dealership.

Vine Wrap Up

Vine, like Instagram, is a place where creativity dominates the landscape. The more creative and entertaining the Vine, the more likes and re-Vines you will get. The interesting part that Vine adds is in the efficiency in which you have to get your point across, because you only have six seconds.

Also, like Instagram, Vine allows for the ability to sync up to other, more popular, forms of social media such as Facebook and Twitter. Because these two applications have been around longer and companies typically have more followers on them, your audience will be bigger, which will hopefully translate into more business for you and your dealership.

Because Vine is one of the fastest growing social media apps out there, good Vines that are creative will get noticed and your business will increase. One needs to look no further than what Dunkin' Donuts and Trident gum have already done by creating commercials. Social media is the Generation Y way of marketing and the marketing tactic of the future and the video capability of Vine has only added to it. It is important to take advantage of this fact and use Vine to its true potential, which will turn more business for you and your dealership.

SUMMARY

Having a successful strategy for reaching millennials is becoming important with each passing day. In many ways, millennials are different than previous generations. Studies show car buying and driving habits of millennials to be considerably different compared to previous generations, which makes understanding millennials even more challenging.

Instagram and Vine are two fast-growing social media channels embraced by millennials. If you are new to these channels, spend some time to learn more on how to use these resources to increase your sales, and how they can benefit your dealership and brand. Having a sound understanding of how these two social media applications can benefit your dealership will allow for you to utilize them in the most efficient and creative way possible. We hope you will find our suggestions and tips to be helpful in your quest to effectively reach millennials.

WARNING — DISCLAIMER

This book is designed to provide information on marketing, promoting and the overall usability of social media for auto dealers. It is sold or given with the understanding that the publisher and authors are not engaged in rendering legal, accounting or other professional services. If legal or other expert assistance is required, the services of a competent professional should be sought. It is not the purpose of this manual to reprint all the information that is otherwise available to auto dealers, but instead to complement, amplify and supplement other texts. You are urged to read all the available material, learn as much as possible about social media, and tailor the information to your individual needs. For more information, you may write to the publishing company or refer to the official website located at: http://www.DoNascimento.com/Books.

Anyone who decides to use this book must expect to invest a lot of time and effort into it. For many people, social media is more lucrative than other marketing channels and many have built solid, growing, rewarding businesses using new media.

Every effort has been made to make this manual as complete and accurate as possible.

However, there may be errors, both typographical and in content. Therefore, this text should be used only as a general guide and not as the ultimate source of social media marketing information. Furthermore, this manual contains information on social media that is current only up to the printing date.

The purpose of this manual is to educate and entertain. The authors and publishing company shall have neither liability nor responsibility to any person or entity with respect to any loss or damage caused, or alleged to have been caused, directly or indirectly, by the information contained in this book.

If you do not wish to be bound by the above, you may return this book to the publisher with a proof of purchase receipt for a full refund.

DoNascimento.com/Books
Publisher